Introduction to AutoLISP

P. M. Moanfeldt
Gateway Community-Technical College

Prentice Hall
Upper Saddle River, New Jersey   Columbus, Ohio

Library of Congress Cataloging-in-Publication Data

Moanfeldt, P. M.
    Introduction to AutoLISP / P. M. Moanfeldt.
        p.   cm.
    Includes index.
    ISBN 0-13-206624-6
    1. AutoLISP (Computer program language)   I. Title.
QA76.73.A84M63   1997
620' .0042' 02855369—dc20

96-30974
CIP

Editor: Stephen Helba
Production Editor: Linda Hillis Bayma
Production Coordination: Custom Editorial Productions, Inc.
Cover Designer: Proof Positive/Farrowlyne Assoc., Inc.
Cover Design Coordinator: Karrie M. Converse
Production Manager: Laura Messerly
Marketing Manager: Frank Mortimer, Jr.

This book was set in Times Roman by Custom Editorial Productions, Inc. and was printed and bound by Book Press, Inc., a Quebecor America Book Group Company. The cover was printed by Phoenix Color Corp.

 © 1997 by Prentice-Hall, Inc.
Simon & Schuster/A Viacom Company
Upper Saddle River, New Jersey 07458

Printed in the United States of America.

10 9 8 7 6 5 4 3 2 1

ISBN 0-13-206624-6

Prentice-Hall International (UK) Limited, *London*
Prentice-Hall of Australia Pty. Limited, *Sydney*
Prentice-Hall Canada Inc., *Toronto*
Prentice-Hall Hispanoamericana, S. A., *Mexico*
Prentice-Hall of India Private Limited, *New Delhi*
Prentice-Hall of Japan, Inc., *Tokyo*
Simon & Schuster Asia Pte. Ltd., *Singapore*
Editora Prentice-Hall do Basil, Ltda., *Rio de Jeneiro*

To my wife, Carol, who, in spite of the fact that she dislikes computers almost as much as she does cats, patiently sat and allowed me to discuss the book with her, and who offered suggestions that immeasurably improved this book's organization.

PREFACE

AutoCAD is a very powerful, flexible program. It can work effectively in any drafting discipline, as well as in a number of fields not usually thought of as being involved with drafting. But AutoCAD pays a price for its flexibility. Because it has so many capabilities, it must have a great many options. This means that users may have to go through several layers of options to accomplish a given task. AutoCAD's default options reduce this problem somewhat, but what if the user prefers a different approach? To take a trivial example, anyone who usually draws circles by specifying three points is doomed to have to continually enter "3P" instead being able to take advantage of the default of directly selecting the circle's center.

The bottom line is: If you know enough AutoCAD to do something, you can learn to write an AutoLISP program to do it even faster and with less effort.

Who (in addition to those who like to draw three-point circles) would be interested in learning AutoLISP? I think that this population falls into the following four groups:

- Drafters who use AutoCAD for repetitive tasks.
- Drafters who dislike having to work through AutoCAD options.
- Individuals who want to improve their knowledge of AutoCAD and how it works.
- Experimenters who wish to combine drafting automation with a degree of flexibility.

Whatever your reasons for learning AutoLISP, you'll find there's a great deal of satisfaction in having a program work that you designed. It counteracts the hands-on feel missing from AutoCAD as compared to conventional drafting. When working with AutoLISP, you know that you're in command, not a computer. If you run into a problem, it's up to you to work it out.

This book essentially deals with the AutoLISP supplied with AutoCAD's version 12. The AutoLISP supplied with AutoCAD version 13 contains additional commands that deal primarily with exterior programs, that is, commands not primarily concerned with the production of drawings. Therefore, since AutoLISP has been a feature of AutoCAD since version 2.18, it's probably a good idea to check each function for compatibility if you're working with an earlier version. The programs and program fragments in this text will generally work with any AutoLISP version. AutoCAD's prompt sequences, however, change from version to version, so anything in the **command** function should be checked against the AutoCAD version in use.

A good working knowledge of AutoCAD is a critical requirement for success in AutoLISP. You don't need to know all the AutoCAD commands and options or be able to visualize the AutoCAD solution to any given problem from scratch. You do need a general knowledge of AutoCAD, being able to roughly figure out how to solve a given problem with AutoCAD, and have access to AutoCAD's documentation or a good textbook so as to be able to review the more esoteric options.

This book is intended to be an introductory survey, so several areas of AutoLISP have been omitted: the **boole, trace** and **untrace** functions, functions for stepping through the subentities of polylines and blocks, graphics functions dealing with direct communication with the monitor, all functions dealing with extended entity data, and many functions dealing with memory usage. Any functions added to version 13 that deal with the basic AutoCAD program have been included in the discussion, except those dealing with external programs such as ASE, ASX, Diesel, Programmable Dialog Boxes, database linkage, and other areas which don't directly relate to the interaction of AutoCAD and AutoLISP. The book is set up in terms of concepts, rather than in order of increasing complexity. This means that all the functions dealing with a given area of AutoLISP are grouped together, even though some of them are more advanced than others.

Many sample programs and fragments are included in the text. The latter may be written at the Command: line from within AutoCAD or as mini programs on a word processor accessed through the SH or SHELL commands. If the system permits, longer programs may also be written without exiting AutoCAD by shelling out to a word processor.

Several typographical conventions are used in this book to alleviate the confusion between AutoCAD and AutoLISP functions. In the text, AutoCAD commands are written in uppercase (e.g., LINE) and command options are written with an initial capital letter (e.g., Window). AutoLISP functions are in lowercase bold type (e.g., **getpoint**) and generic sections of AutoLISP programs are written in bold with an initial capital letter (e.g., **Then**). When program variables are used in text discussions, they are shown in italic uppercase letters (e.g., *OUTPUT*).

Inside the example programs and fragments, AutoCAD commands, variables, and options begin with an uppercase letter. Functions are in lowercase, but not bold.

In actual use, neither AutoCAD commands nor AutoLISP programs are case-sensitive. For example, the AutoCAD regeneration command could be written as regen, REGEN, or even RegEN. Similarly, AutoLISP code may be written in uppercase, lowercase, or a mixture of both.

Keyboard entries in the text are printed between quotes. When more than one pair of quotes is present, only the outer pair should be omitted. For example, "(load "A:TRY")" should be entered as (load "A:TRY").

A few final words about the exercises at the end of each chapter. DO THEM! Even if you think you know the point of the exercise, it will help you to work your way through them. If possible, do the work on a computer by typing at the AutoCAD command line. That way, you'll not only check out the exercise, you'll get hands-on experience with computing. While you're at it, try a little experimentation on your own. Use your own variables, make up your own lists and tear them apart, and try a little programming. Even if you're not successful on the first try, you'll have gained experience in AutoLISP thinking that will pay off later.

Look at the discussions of the exercises in Appendix B, even if you have successfully gone through the exercises. This section discusses alternate approaches and blind alleys, rather than just list code.

Finally, don't get discouraged if your first efforts don't work out. AutoLISP is a language, just like French, German, and Mandarin. You wouldn't expect to pick up and read a book on beginning French, and then feel comfortable speaking French to a French person. Don't expect to learn even the basics of AutoLISP without running into some difficulties.

The DOS referred to in this text is Microsoft MS–DOS, a copyrighted product of the Microsoft Corp. AutoCAD and AutoLISP are trademarks of Autodesk Inc., which has given me permission to use the material in Appendix A.

Acknowledgments

This book could not have been written without the support of my family, who put up with my absences while I was writing, and my presence whenever I ran into a sticking point.

I'd also like to thank my colleagues in the Engineering Technology Department of Gateway Community-Technical College for letting me bounce my ideas off them.

And a special thanks to the plank-holders at what is now Midlands Technical College, Columbia, South Carolina, for showing me what good teaching is all about.

Specific thanks must go to Rob Wahl, Gateway's director of computer services, who repeatedly brought back my files after I pushed the wrong key, and to the following individuals who offered corrections and suggestions: Kevin Downs, Lancaster Vocational Technical school; Steven Dulmes, College of Lake County; Louis D. Lauritzen, Texas State Technical College; and C. Ed Margraff, Marion Technical College.

All that is good in this book is due to them. The rest is my responsibility.

P. M. Moanfeldt, Ph.D.

CONTENTS

LIST OF TABLES

LIST OF ILLUSTRATIONS

LIST OF MAJOR PROGRAMS

CHAPTER 1

The Basics of AutoLISP

OBJECTIVES

After reading this chapter, you will be able to:

*   Identify atoms and lists in AutoLISP.
*   Specify and give examples of the three basic types of data recognized by AutoLISP.
*   Create lists with the *cons, list, quote,* or *reverse* functions.
*   Extract atoms and lists using the *car, cdr* (and their derivatives), *last,* and *nth* functions.
*   Use *getxx* functions to assign values to variables from the keyboard.

1.1   LISTS IN AUTOLISP

LISP (*LISt Processor*) is a programming language that was originally developed for use in artificial intelligence work. Because it was so adaptable, it soon found uses in other fields. AutoLISP is an enhanced subset of LISP commands. The enhancement involves the addition of several commands from AutoCAD to a selection of the basic LISP commands. These additional commands enable AutoLISP to react with the AutoCAD drawing editor, thus controlling the development of a drawing. Although it is a very powerful tool, AutoLISP retains the basic simplicity of the parent LISP so it can be used to perform repetitive drafting procedures with little or no assistance from the computer operator.

1

As might be gathered from their names, both LISP and AutoLISP deal with lists. These lists are defined as a collection of individual items (called *atoms*) grouped inside a pair of parentheses (). The number of items may range upward from 0 (the null list), but most of the simple lists dealt with in AutoLISP arc lcss than a dozen items long. The list may contain AutoLISP functions, numbers, variable names, strings, or even other lists (in which case the first list is a compound or complex list rather than a simple one). Below are some examples of AutoLISP lists.

A seven-atom list of numbers:

```
(1 3 5 3 6 7 89073)
```

A five-atom list containing a list and strings:

```
((2 3) "TOM" "dick" "HaRRY" "Bogart and Bacall")
```

A four-atom list containing an AutoLISP function, the addition operator, and numbers:

```
(+ 2 3 27)
```

Almost anything can be included in a list. From a practical standpoint, the lists used in AutoLISP must be internally consistent. A list such as:

```
(+ "TOM" "HARRY")
```

wouldn't make sense, since the quotation marks around TOM and HARRY signify that they are nonnumerical strings and can't be added. On the other hand:

```
(- joe pete)
```

would make sense if *joe* and *pete* represented integer or real numerical values.

Many of the lists encountered in AutoLISP are point lists. These consist of two or three digits that specify the Cartesian coordinates of points in the current user coordinate system.

In AutoLISP, most simple lists consist of either data or an AutoLISP function or operator followed by the appropriate data. These simple lists can be combined to form compound lists, the same way lines of BASIC, COBOL, or FORTRAN code can be combined to form complex programs.

1.2   SPACES AND PUNCTUATION

Before going any further in our discussion, it might be a good idea to go over some of AutoLISP's ground rules. Look back at the lists we were just discussing. Notice anything? There weren't any commas separating the atoms. That's because AutoLISP can use stand-alone spaces to separate items. It doesn't matter how many spaces are between a pair of items. This means that you can use as many spaces as you want to between items to make the program easier for humans to read. Extra spaces *should* be avoided between double quotation marks—but only for aesthetic reasons—because everything between double quotes is treated literally, and parroted back without any attempt to interpret it.

Line returns, however, are significant—at least when you are writing AutoLISP from the AutoCAD command line while inside the drawing editor. At the command line, AutoLISP interprets a line return (or hitting the "Enter" key) as the termination of whatever code you're writing. So unless you really wish to terminate coding, keep away from the return key. On the other hand, you can keep typing at the end of a line on the screen, and the text will simply scroll down to the next line. If you are writing code outside the drawing editor, line returns are permissible, but if they're between double quotes, spaces will show up the on the screen, possibly distorting text material. Don't have blank lines in front of or inside your code: be sure to put something on each line, even if it is only a single closing parenthesis or semicolon.[1]

Parentheses probably cause more trouble than anything else in AutoLISP. Lists must be enclosed in parentheses, and everything in AutoLISP is a list. Therefore, an AutoLISP program will have a lot of parentheses. Programs may have many levels of lists; that is, a list may be inside another list which, in turn, is inside a third list, and so on. The beginning and end of each of these lists is denoted by an opening or a closing parentheses, and the program will not run unless we have the right number of parentheses, correctly placed. Later on, we'll see how to keep track of parentheses, but for the moment, just remember that is important to place them properly. AutoLISP doesn't normally require spaces in front of or behind parentheses (the parentheses themselves serve to separate atoms), but from a readability standpoint, it is a good idea to set them off with leading and trailing spaces.

AutoLISP reserves a few other characters for special purposes. The single quote (') is used as an alternative to the **quote** function, which will be discussed later in this chapter. The period (.) is used as a decimal point or to form a special type of list called a "dotted pair" (in either case, there must be a character both in front of and behind the period). The semicolon (;) and combinations of the semicolon and the vertical line character (;| or |;) identify AutoLISP comments. Anything in a comment, including other punctuation marks, is ignored by AutoLISP. In contrast, material between double quotes is not evaluated, but used verbatim in the program.

The characters listed below:

$$* = - + < > /$$

are used for math or logical functions, and should not be used elsewhere. The backslash (\) is used in formatting output, and by DOS, so it, too, shouldn't be used unless needed.

---

[1]Anything on a line following a semicolon is treated as a comment by AutoLISP and ignored.

Parentheses, single and double quotes, the comment characters, and (except when used in the drawing editor) line returns terminate symbols and numerical constants, so they may be used in addition to, or in place of spaces. From the standpoint of readability (by humans, not the computer) spaces are preferable.

1.3   DATA TYPES

Most computer programs need data input while running if they are to do anything useful. AutoLISP will accept data from the keyboard, from the screen, or from data files. Although all data will ultimately be represented by a string of zeros and ones, AutoLISP requires that a distinction be made between data types when programming or entering data from the keyboard.

Three basic types of data are recognized by AutoLISP: real numbers, integers, and strings. These three types of data enable the computer operator to communicate with the program and control its flow. Understanding what the different types of data are and how they operate is necessary for efficient and effective programming.

A real number is a set of digits, optionally preceded by a plus or a minus sign and containing a decimal point. The decimal point must have at least one digit in front of it, and one behind. Real numbers may also be expressed in exponential notation in the form:

```
NNNe+/-nn
```

where NNN can be any number of digits, e (or E) is the exponentiation symbol, and nn any positive or negative digits from 0 to 99 (if nn is omitted, NNN will be returned). The decimal point is optional in NNN but, if present, it must be preceded by at least one leading digit. Both AutoCAD and AutoLISP use real numbers for distances, dimensions, specifying points on the screen, angles of rotation, etc.

Valid Real Numbers	Invalid Real Numbers	
	Number	Reason
27.3	273	No decimal point
–0.3	.875	No digit in front of the decimal point
+97.63	45.	No trailing digit
15.5E–09	.155E	No leading digit
0.234e+12	1,256	Comma not permitted

Integers are whole numbers. They cannot have decimals, or, when divided, remainders (2/3 = 0, 3/2 = 1). Integers may have leading + or – signs, but not commas. If AutoLISP encounters a positive or negative with an absolute value integer greater than approximately 2E+09, it converts it to a real number. In addition, Version 12 AutoCAD cannot handle integers with absolute values greater than about 32000. Integers are used by AutoCAD and AutoLISP in counting situations. Examples include: the number of times a group of AutoLISP lists is repeated within a program, the number of rows in an ARRAY command, the number of sections a line will be partitioned into with the DIVIDE command, and the number of commands removed by UNDO.

Valid Integers	Invalid Integers	
	Integer	Reason
32	35.0	No decimal points permitted
–123	1,234	No commas permitted
+426	3E+02	Exponential form not allowed

To put it simply, a string is any printable character (including numbers and spaces) or characters enclosed between two sets of double quotes. Strings are used for text input; for naming drawings, AutoCAD commands, and options; and for string and numerical default values at the command line.

Valid Strings	Invalid Strings	
	String	Reason
"27"	27	No quotation marks
"Yes"	"Yes	No trailing quotes
"Thirty-two"	'Circle'	Must be double quotes
"@#$%^%"	" "Boy" "	Too many quotes
"Now is the time!"	to act"	No leading quotes

Data that is embodied in the program code has to be of the correct type and in the correct form for its type. In other words, strings must be between quotes, reals must have embedded decimals, and integers can have signs but no decimal points. Failure to follow these conventions will produce programming errors that are difficult to track down. Fortunately, once located, they are easy to correct!

The rules on the types (but not the forms) of data are relaxed for keyboard input. The AutoLISP functions that accept data while a program is running are relatively tolerant. If a string is being called for and the integer value 27 is keyed in, it will be converted to the string value "27". If a real is expected, 27 will be converted to 27.0. But this flexibility comes at a price: if a string is expected and the correctly formatted string "27" is keyed in, AutoLISP will treat it as ""27"" which is usually invalid input.

If a string is keyed in when either real or integer input is expected, the input value will not be accepted and the operator will be prompted to submit a numerical value. If a real is entered when an integer is expected, the prompt will be "Requires an integer value."

Point lists are composed of real numbers. If integers are programmed in or entered from the keyboard, they will be converted to reals. Points are entered from the keyboard in response to AutoLISP prompts just as they are for AutoCAD prompts; that is, separated by commas and *not* between parentheses. AutoLISP will convert such entries into two or three member lists. Points specified in the program code must be in the form of lists. Formation of lists with the **quote**, ', or **list** functions is discussed below.

1.4   FUNCTIONS

In order to eliminate a great deal of repetitive coding, AutoLISP supplies the programmer with 179 predefined functions (and one predefined constant, **pi** = 3.1415. . .). These functions not only make programming possible, they also make it faster and easier. From the standpoint of the beginning programmer, functions also provide a common ground for understanding other programmers' work.

Think of a function as a sort of black box that accepts data as input, does something to it, then returns the data in a modified form. As an example, suppose a variable called *COUNT* currently has a value of 7. If we submit *COUNT* to the + function in the form of the list:

```
(+ count 3)
```

the function would return the value of ten. (*COUNT*, though, would still be 7—the + function does not change its value.) The value returned could be used as the input to another function.

Most programs require more than one function to accomplish their tasks, so AutoLISP's function library also includes a function to make other functions. These new functions (called user-defined functions—UDFs for short) are one of the best justifications for learning AutoLISP. By stringing functions together, a programmer can produce a UDF that will accomplish a complex task with a minimum of user input and effort.

Functions or, more properly, function lists may contain arguments, symbols, flags, messages, and/or other functions. Depending on the function, any or all of these may either be optional or required. Like most programming languages, AutoLISP is unforgiving about the form of a function. Misspell the name of a function, omit a required argument, or put any of the modifiers in the wrong place and the program will crash. A formal definition of all the AutoLISP functions is included in Appendix A.

Arguments supply data from outside the function for the function to work on. Inside the function, symbols are used to represent the quantities that are to be manipulated by the function. When present, flags (which may be thought of as dummy variables with the usual value being either "T" or "nil") may be used as toggles or to select between various options within a function. Messages are almost always optional, but should be used whenever the opportunity arises. They allow the function to tell the user what has happened (e.g., "File not found") or, more often, what the user is supposed to do at a particular point (e.g., "Enter the bolt diameter:") With one class of exceptions, AutoLISP will print out whatever is in a message without doing anything to it, so spelling *doesn't* count—except, possibly, to the user. The exceptions to the "What AutoLISP sees is what it prints!" rule are the combination of certain characters with the backslash (\). One of the most useful of these combinations is \n, the code for a line feed. It will print your message at the extreme left of a new line. A message printed on its own line will stand out from the clutter on the Command: line and is easier to spot and to understand.

Let's take a look at a function in action to understand how the different parts of the function list are used. Consider the functions embodied in the list below:

```
(setq a (getstring F "\n Enter your full name: "))
```

The line includes two lists. The inner list is

```
(getstring F "\n Enter your full name: ")
```

while the outer list has three items: **setq**, a, and the inner list.

Setq is a function. It sets the second atom, *a*, to the value of the string returned by the inner list. **Getstring** is another function. It returns the user's response to the prompt as a string. "F" is a flag. When used with **getstring** (and provided it has been assigned any value but "nil" by a previous **setq**), it will allow **getstring** to accept spaces in the user supplied input. If the flag is missing or set to "nil," a space will act just as it does in AutoCAD and terminate the entry. Many programmers prefer to use "T" as the value for this type of flag, since the computer is really asking "Is a flag present?" If it is, the answer is *True*.

The material between the double quotes is the message. Since the message is the only way the programmer has to communicate with a user, some thought must devoted to its contents. In this case, the apparently simple message embodies the unspoken assumptions that the user knows enough to put a space between his or her first and last name and hit the return key to complete the entry. If either of these assumptions were wrong, a different message would be needed.

If any single function can lay claim to being the most important to AutoLISP, it is probably the **command** function. **Command** links AutoCAD to AutoLISP and allows the AutoLISP programmer to think in terms of doing something to a drawing with AutoCAD instead of starting from scratch. As Figure 1.1 shows, the function starts with the word "command," followed by an AutoCAD command in quotes,

(command "PLINE" p1 "W" 0 ".5" pause "")
   Ⓐ   ⒷⒸⒹⒺ Ⓕ Ⓖ

A AutoCAD command (see note below)

B Variable representing a point defined in
   a previous AutoLISP statement

C AutoCAD command option (see note below)

D AutoLISP value

E AutoCAD value—zero not required
   before or after decimal points

F AutoLISP instruction

G AutoCAD return, to exit command

Note: AutoCAD commands and options may be
in either upper- or lowercase.

FIGURE 1.1   Anatomy of the Command Function.

followed by AutoCAD options (also in quotes), AutoLISP defined variables, and numerical data.

Although the AutoLISP form of a given command is similar to the AutoCAD form, it differs in some important respects. In AutoLISP:

- All AutoCAD commands and options must be between double quotes.

- Commands must be spelled out in full, although the options may use AutoCAD aliases.

- AutoLISP does not use explicit returns after each entry (although the spaces could be thought of as "returns").

- User input must be specified by inserting PAUSE (no quotes) in the appropriate place in the function list for each required input. (If AutoCAD is expecting a string input when PAUSE is invoked, the system variable *TEXTEVAL* must be set to a nonzero value; otherwise, PAUSE would be taken as the expected input.)

- In situations where AutoCAD requires a return to terminate a command or selection, AutoLISP uses a pair of double quotes.

- Decimals in AutoLISP must have both leading and trailing numerical characters. If the decimals are between quotes, they are treated as AutoCAD, rather than AutoLISP, input, so a less restrictive format may be used and leading/trailing characters need not be present. Table 1.1 gives guidelines for AutoCAD and AutoLISP numerical input to AutoLISP.

- Finally, default values should not be assumed in AutoLISP usage of AutoCAD commands. With AutoCAD, the operator can see the value for a default and change it if necessary. In AutoLISP, this opportunity doesn't exist, so the value should be explicitly set.

1.4.1 Variables and Values

Like most computer languages, AutoLISP uses variables as symbols to represent specific values. These variables are manipulated by various mathematical and logical processes, and the values assigned to them change accordingly. Since the variables stand in for values, they can supply input to AutoCAD commands just as well as the equivalent numbers or strings can. Unless otherwise instructed, whenever a variable is encountered by an AutoLISP program, it is evaluated and the current value is "returned," so that its value is made available to the next step in the program.

Unlike many other computer languages, there are no requirements for associating the variable names to the types of the values they represent. A given AutoLISP variable could represent a real number, an integer, a string, or a list. Any combination of upper- or lowercase letters or numbers may be used as a variable name, but spaces are not allowed and neither are most punctuation marks. Some combinations, although permissible, should be avoided.

TABLE 1.1 AutoCAD and AutoLISP Numerical Input to AutoLISP

Type	AutoLISP Acceptable	AutoLISP Unacceptable	AutoCAD Acceptable
Integer	27	325.0	"15"
Real	17.0	21.*	"25"* or "17.2"
Real	0.123	.456	".5"

*Whole numbers with no significant decimal digits and no trailing decimal are accepted as input to **command** and **getreal** functions.

A few suggestions about variable names follow:

- Using the name of an AutoCAD function as a symbol name will redefine the function, leading to unexpected—and usually undesirable—results.

- Keeping symbol names short reduces keyboarding time. In addition, symbols longer than six characters drastically increase the demands on the limited amount of memory space AutoLISP allocates for symbol storage.

- The use of allowable punctuation marks in symbol names leads to confusion when reading them. On the other hand, some programmers preface certain types of symbols with a punction mark (e.g., #point1) as protection against confusing the symbol with those used by third-party programs.

Linking or binding AutoLISP symbols to their values is done with an assignment statement. AutoLISP has three types of assignment functions, shown in Table 1.2.

Setq assigns a string or expression to a variable. It is the basic AutoLISP assignment function. The "q" in **setq** could stand for the embedded AutoLISP function **quote**. Whatever atom or list follows **quote** (or its equivalent, ') is treated literally by AutoLISP. In the absence of **quote**, AutoLISP will attempt to evaluate the following atom or list; that is, treat it as a variable with an assigned value. By embodying the **quote** function, **setq** can treat the immediately following atom as a literal label and make it the variable name for the third term in the sequence. When a variable is encountered in a program after it has been assigned a value with **setq**, the variable is evaluated and replaced by its current value. Consider the examples below:

```
(setq a 3)
(setq b "hArrY")
(setq c (list 2 3))
```

In each of these lists, the second atom in the list becomes an AutoLISP symbol or variable, and the third atom is the value assigned to the symbol. Therefore, the three lists above set *A* to the integer value 3, *B* to the string "hArrY", and *C* to the list (2 3).

TABLE 1.2   Assignment Functions

Function	Notes
(set 'a b 'c d . . .)	Sets 'a (must be quoted) to value of b, 'c to d . . .
(setq a b c d . . .)	Sets a to b, c to d . . .
(setvar "sysvar" a)	Sets quoted system variable to a

To conserve memory space, multiple **setq** statements may be stacked, as shown below:

```
(setq a 3 b "hArrY" c (list 2 3))
```

Here, the second, fourth, and sixth atoms are the variables, and the third, fifth, and seventh atoms are the values to be assigned. As far as the results go, the two methods are equivalent, but the second conserves both memory space and keyboarding effort.

Lacking the built-in quote, the **set** function evaluates the second item in a list (unless it has a quotation mark in front of it) and returns its value. In other words

```
(setq a 3)
```

and

```
(set 'a 3)
```

are equivalent. But whereas

```
(setq b a)
```

would set the value of *B* to 3 and return 3,

```
(set b a)
```

would not, returning an error message instead, because *B* would be evaluated (probably returning nil) and *A* would be an extra atom in the list.

The **set** function is generally used in complex expressions, where the atom immediately following **set** is another AutoCAD function instead of an undefined variable. **Set** will be more fully discussed in a later chapter. However, before leaving **set**, you need to be aware that it can indirectly assign a value to a variable as in the following sequence:

```
(setq r 3) or (set 'r 3)
(setq s 'r) or (set 's 'r)
(set s 5)
```

The first line sets *R* to 3, the second sets *S* to *R* without evaluating the latter, and the third line sets *S* to 5. Note that *S* is not quoted in the third line, so it is evaluated and the expression returns *R*, and sets *R* to 5! This could lead to problems. If (set s 5) did not immediately follow the second line, the value of *R* could be changed without the programmer realizing it. You can avoid this problem by always using **setq**, unless you need the special properties of **set**.

Setvar is a specialized function used only to assign values to AutoCAD system variables.

```
(setvar "SNAPUNIT" (list 2 3))
```

would set the variable *SNAPUNIT* (which controls values for SNAP) so that the user had a two-unit snap horizontally, and a three-unit snap vertically.

1.4.2   Making and Breaking Lists

There are two basic ways to make a normal list. Consider two compound lists assigned to the variables *A* and *B*:

```
(setq a (list 1 (2 3) 4 5))
(setq b '(6 (7 8) 9 10))
```

If either of the above statements are entered at the command line of an AutoCAD drawing, the appropriate list will be returned on the following line. If, at a later time, while still in the drawing, "!a" or "!b" is entered (without the quotation marks), the associated list will again be returned. Entering any defined AutoLISP symbol at the drawing editor command line prefaced by an exclamation mark will return the current value. This supplies a quick and easy way of verifying the current values of AutoLISP variables.

   If the list is to only consist of numbers, either method will do the job, but if the list contains symbols, use of the quote will prevent their evaluation. So, if the *values* of the symbols are desired, the first method must be used to build the list.

   Consider the following:

```
(setq a 1)
(setq b (list a 2 3))
(setq c '(a 2 3))
```

Entering "!b" from the command line will return (1 2 3), but "!c" will yield (a 2 3). In other words, the **list** approach evaluates any variables and returns their values, while the **quote** approach does not.

   Whenever a point must be supplied to AutoCAD, a two- or three-atom list or an equivalent variable would constitute valid input. The following example illustrates the use of AutoLISP from the command line (user responses are underlined):

```
LINE <RET>
From: !p1 <RET>
To: !p2 <RET> <RET>
```

If both P1 and P2 have previously been defined as two- (2-D) or three- (3-D) atom lists, a line will be drawn from the coordinates represented by P1 to those represented by P2.

   Two other functions are available to make lists. The **reverse** function, as its name implies, will reverse the order of a list. For example:

```
(setq a (list 1 2 "BOY"))
(setq b (reverse a))
```

will return ("BOY" 2 1).

   The **cons** function will add an atom or a list to an existing atom or list. Assume that *A* has previously been defined as (1 2 3) and *B* represents the list (4 5 6). Then

```
(cons 0 a)
```

returns (0 1 2 3) and

```
(cons b a)
```

returns ((4 5 6) 1 2 3).[2]

Table 1.3 summarizes the four list creation functions. There are times, though, when lists have to be broken apart. Consider the problem of using AutoLISP to draw a rectangle that is defined by two points, one at a lower corner, and the other at the opposite upper corner (the way a Window or Crossing box is defined). Picking the lower-left and upper-right corners will give two of the necessary four points. The other two corners have yet to be defined. Even so, we know the coordinates of the missing corners. The lower-right corner has the X coordinate of the upper-right corner and the Y coordinate of the lower-left corner. The upper-left corner has the same X coordinate as the lower-left point and the same Y coordinate as the upper-right point.

Clearly, although the first two picks gave us all the information needed to construct the rectangle, the coordinate lists must be rearranged to get the missing coordinate pairs. Four basic functions, summarized in Table 1.4, are available for this purpose.

The **car** function returns the first item on the list (usually an atom, but occasionally a list), while **cdr** yields a list consisting of everything in the original list *except* the first item. For example, assume that *L1* is a list consisting of (1 2 3 4 5) and *L2* a list consisting of ((1 2) 3 4 5). **Car** *L1* would be:

```
1
```

while **cdr** *L1* would be

```
(2 3 4 5)
```

TABLE 1.3   List Creation Functions

Function	Notes
(cons a lst)*	Adds an atom or list to the front of list *lst*
(list a b . . .)	Strings *a b* . . . together to form a list, evaluates variables
(quote a b . . .) or '(a b . . .)	Strings *a b* . . . together to form a list, does not evaluate variables
(reverse lst)	Returns *lst* in reverse order

*If *a* is an atom, and *lst* is replaced by an atom, a dotted pair is returned.

---

[2]If the second item is *not* a list, **cons** will produce a a "dotted pair," as mentioned above. For example: (cons 0 "CIRCLE") returns the dotted pair (0 ."CIRCLE") and (cons 40 3) produces (40 . 3). In general, dotted pairs may not be used when a function calls for a list.

TABLE 1.4 Basic List Extraction Functions

Function	Notes
(car lst)	The first atom or sublist of list *lst*
(cdr lst)	A list consisting of everything but the first item or sublist of list *lst*
(last lst)	The last atom or sublist of list *lst*
(nth num lst)	Returns num item (starting from zero) from *lst* If num > list length, returns "nil"

If *L2* were substituted for *L1*, **car** would be the list (1 2) and **cdr** would be (3 4 5), also a list. Remember, **car** is usually an atom, but on occasion a list; **cdr** is *always* a list, except for dotted pairs.

Another basic function, **last,** returns the last item in a list. For reasons that will become apparent, **last** is rarely used.

The last list extraction function, **nth**, returns a specified item number from a list, for example:

```
(setq a (list "ONE" 2 3 "FOUR")
b (nth 3 a)
)
```

returns "FOUR". The reason for this rather unexpected result is that **nth** starts its count at zero instead of one. Some of AutoLISP's counting functions start their counts at zero, others at one. It's difficult to remember the class into which any given function falls.

A good rule to follow when using these counting functions is to check them out first with a few lines of coding, such as the ones above. By the way, if you had asked for the fourth item in the example above, AutoLISP would have returned "nil" since the list is only "three" long.

In our rectangle example, if we have explicitly specified the first two corners of the rectangle, we can establish the other two corners of the rectangle using both the X and Y coordinates of the previously selected points. There's no problem with the X coordinates—the **car** function will give them to us—but the Y coordinate is a problem since **cdr** returns a *list* containing the Y coordinate, or, in the 3-D case, the Y and Z coordinates. Since a point list must contain the coordinates as *atoms* not as *lists*, **cdr** would not provide acceptable input. What is needed is a way to pull the first item out of the **cdr** of a point list so that it stands alone. To put it another way, we must split the list produced by the **cdr** of a point list into two components, one containing the first item in the list, and the other a list containing everything *except* the first item. This is exactly what **car** does! Figure 1.2 shows how a rectangle is constructed using the **car** function.

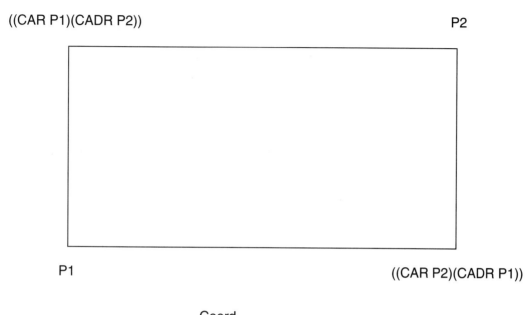

FIGURE 1.2   Construction of a Rectangle.

Variable	Coord. List	CAR	CADR
P1	(1 3)	1	3
P2	(7 6)	7	6

Consider the following coding:

```
1        (setq  e  (list 1 2 3 4)
2               f  (cdr e)
3               g  (car f)
4               h  (cdr f))
5        )
```

Line 2 evaluates to (2 3 4), Line 3 returns Line 2, and Line 4 returns the list (3 4).

When you realize that extracting the X coordinate is simply a matter of calling for **car** *E*, getting the Y (and perhaps the Z) coordinate from a point list appears to be relatively awkward. The task can be simplified by reconsidering the coding.

Line 2 sets *F* to the **cdr** of *E*, and Line 3 sets *G* to the **car** of *F* (which is the same as the **car** of the **cdr** of *E*). AutoLISP permits us to replace Lines 2 and 3 with a single command asking for the **cadr** of *E*. Using the same approach, how could (3 4) be represented with a single **setq** command?

At this point, one might be troubled by visions of long strings of As and Ds bracketed by a C at the front and an R at the rear. Fear not! AutoLISP only allows four levels of this kind of thing, so **caddar** or **cadadr** is OK, but **cadadar** isn't.

Figure 1.3 shows how a five-member list of a sublist and four atoms can be broken down with **car**, **cdr**, and their derivatives. At each level, an atom and a list can be produced without redefining the starting list. If longer lists have to be broken down, other techniques will have to be used.

Using this combined notation, and assuming that X, Y, and Z represent coordinates, if the following holds:

```
(setq p1 (list X Y Z))
```

then the X coordinate of P1 is **car** P1, the Y coordinate of P1 is **cadr** P1, and the Z coordinate of P1 is **caddr** P1.[3]

You can verify this for yourself by typing:

```
(setq p1 (list 1 2 3))
```

at the command line, then hitting the "Enter" key. You should see the list:

```
(1 2 3)
```

appear on the next line. Except for the characters themselves, there's nothing critical except the spaces. There must be one or more spaces between **setq** and P1, between **list** and 1, and between each two of the three numbers and after the first and second numbers. Extra spaces do no harm and, at this stage, readability is preferable to compactness.

Now that you've defined list P1, use **car**, **cdr**, and their derivatives to tear the list apart. Try your hand at constructing lists and extracting terms from them. The ability to extract atoms from lists is very important in AutoLISP, so your time will be well spent.

Now, returning once more to our rectangle, whose lower-left and upper-right corners are represented by lists P1 and P2 respectively, the lower-right corner could be found with:

```
(setq lr (list (car p2) (cadr p1)))
```

and the upper-left with:

```
(setq ul (list (car p1) (cadr p2)))
```

The rectangle could then be drawn by calling up the LINE command, and entering !p1, !lr, !p2, !ul, and C (for close) in response to the prompts.

---

[3]It may seem that **last** could be used to return Y coordinates. This would be unwise, since the last item in a point list could be the Z instead of the Y coordinate. On the other hand, **car**, **cadr**, and **caddr** will always return X, Y, and Z coordinates respectively.

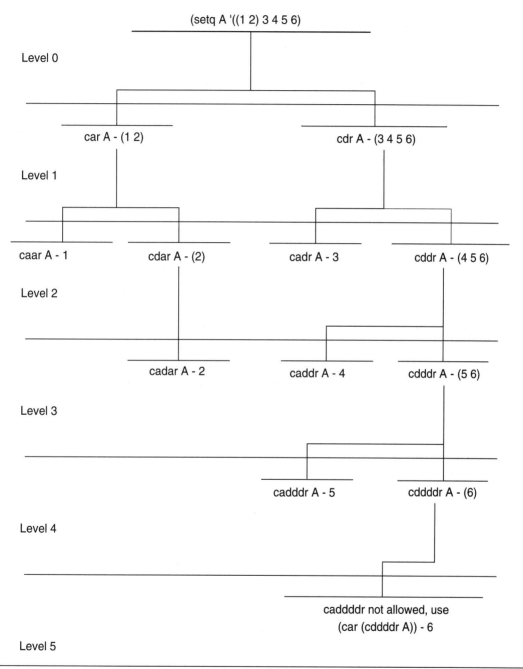

Level 0

car A - (1 2)   cdr A - (3 4 5 6)

Level 1

caar A - 1   cdar A - (2)   cadr A - 3   cddr A - (4 5 6)

Level 2

cadar A - 2   caddr A - 4   cdddr A - (5 6)

Level 3

cadddr A - 5   cddddr A - (6)

Level 4

cadddddr not allowed, use
(car (cddddr A)) - 6

Level 5

FIGURE 1.3   Breaking Down a List.

17

1.4.3 Run Time Input

Using AutoLISP to establish point sets by keying in the **list** function and the desired coordinates when writing code is one of the ways to transfer AutoLISP data to AutoCAD. The problem with this method is that it locks the values into the AutoLISP program. Changing the values of a point set requires the user to access the program, delete the old data, and enter the revised information. Most users are reluctant to go through the procedure. Fortunately, AutoLISP has methods to enter various type of data, including coordinates, from outside the program. The most direct of these methods is through the use of "getxxx" functions, summarized in Table 1.5. The basic format for these functions is:

```
(setq v (getXXX "message"))
```

where "XXX" varies with the type of input required, and the optional message is a prompt telling what the user is to do. Using this method, the data acquisition for the rectangle discussed above could be done as follows:

TABLE 1.5 External Input Functions

Function	Notes
(getangle [pt]) *	Returns angle in radians
(getcorner <pt>) *	Returns box with selected point and *pt* as diagonally opposite corners
(getdist [pt])*	Returns distance between two points
(getenv "var")	Returns string value of system environment variable
(getint) *	Returns integer value
(getkword)	Allows only strings specified by **iniget**
(getorient [pt]) *	Returns angle in current angle units
(getreal) *	Returns real number
(getstring [cr]) *	Returns string, if *cr* present and not nil String may contain spaces
(getvar "var")	Returns value of system variable
(initget [num] [string . . .])	Filters out unacceptable responses for **getkword** and numerical **getxxx** functions
(osnap pt "mode")	Replicates OSNAP with cross hairs at *pt*

Notes: · functions may have prompts for program users; [ ] optional term; < > required term.

```
(setq LL (getpoint "Pick lower-left-hand corner: ")
      UR (getpoint "Pick upper-right-hand corner: ")
      LR (list (car ur)(cdr LL))
      UL (list (car LL)(cdr ur)
)
```

Except for the **getvar** and **getenv** functions—which are not true—**getxxx** functions only accept inputs from AutoCAD and the operating system. All the getXXX functions can have optional messages. Although optional to AutoLISP, these messages are critical to the programmer since they provide an effective way to communicate with the user. The content of these messages should be carefully thought out, preferably with the aid of a nonprogrammer using the program for the first time.

Although the **getxxx** functions will only accept specific types of input (e.g., anything entered in response to **getstring** will be converted into a string, and any number entered in response to **getint** will be converted to an integer), they cannot control the content of the entry. Suppose **getint** were used to find out how many times a particular operation is to be repeated and the value entered is a negative number. The programmer must either add the coding to cope with this type of entry, have the program crash, or provide some mechanism to allow only certain types of integers to be acceptable responses.

The **initget** function provides such a mechanism, and when used with the **getkword** function, it can also control string input.

Neither **initget** nor the **initget/getkword** combination should be used during the initial stages of programming. If anybody knows what input is expected by the program, surely it is the programmer who is doing the coding. Once the program is properly functioning and ready to be used by third parties this type of input control should be considered. The use of **initget** and **getkword** will be fully discussed in a later chapter.

In addition to the limited input controls offered by the **getxxx** functions, once a variable is assigned a value, the variable can be given various logical tests to eliminate many types of unsuitable entry. But as long as the programmer permits the user to enter data from the keyboard, it is impossible to completely prevent unsuitable entries. Good prompts can guide the legitimate user, but if someone is determined to crash a program, a way can be found to make it crash. The only thing a programmer can find comfort in is the fact that the worst thing that can happen is that the user may have to reboot the system.

EXERCISES

Remember, AutoLISP expressions must be in the form of lists enclosed in parentheses. To see what a given expression returns, enter the expression at the Command: prompt in AutoCAD. To see what the value of a variable is, enter an exclamation point, then the variable (no parentheses). The answers for all these exercises are given in the back of this book. The answers include a discussion of each exercise—even if you got the answers correct, the discussion may be worthwhile.

1. Using AutoLISP, write the code to instruct the computer to draw a vertical line from PT1 to PT2 and make 12 copies of it equally spaced in a circle with PT1 as the center of the circle.

2. Given the list ("ART" "bob" chuck D2) which is assigned to the variable *A*, show the functions that will isolate each of the atoms using only **car**, **cdr**, and their derivatives.

3. Given the list *B* containing points 1,2,3 and 4,5,6, extract the X, Y, and Z coordinates of each point using only **car**, **cdr**, and their derivatives.

4. Suppose you have a "long" list, say (Sun Mon Tue Wed Thu Fri Sat) assigned to variable *C*. Extract each entry *without* using the derivatives of **car** and **cdr**.

5. Indicate whether each of the variables below is valid (V); valid, but probably should be avoided (A); or satisfactory (OK).

list	lst	&list	AplusB	A+B	A_B	NEWLIST
POINT1	PT1	CIRCLE	DiA	OLST	Num(1)	
FIVE%						

6. The data entries below are either valid reals, strings, or integers or they are invalid. If they're valid, indicate their types with R, S, or I; if they're invalid, explain why.

```
27    "27"   "TWENTY-SEVEN"   27.0   .27e+02    27.    27E-2
270/10
"TWENNY-SEVEN AND A HALF"          (27)
```

7. Make the letters *A–E* variables and assign the values 1–5 to them respectively.

8. Redo Exercise 7 if you haven't done it during this session. Using two different techniques, make a list containing the letters *A–E* as individual entities.

9. The system variables *SNAPMODE* and *GRIDMODE* have values of 1 or 0. Using AutoLISP, set their values to 1.

10. Using a **getxxx** function, construct a statement that will assign your full name to the variable *NAME*.

11. Enter **getint**, **getreal**, and **getstring** by typing each function at the command line between parentheses with a dummy prompt—for example (getstring "T "). Then

strike the Enter key. At the prompt, enter each of the following values in turn: .3, 27, two. Before striking the Enter key to have the function act on your input, try to predict what will happen. Check your predictions against the output (the first atom that appears is your data entry, the second is the value returned by AutoLISP).

CHAPTER 2

More on Data

OBJECTIVES

After reading this chapter, you will be able to:

- Use arithmetic operators to change the values of variables representing numerical quantities.
- Use logical operators to evaluate expressions containing string variables and values.
- Use logical operators to evaluate expressions containing numerical variables and values.
- Use test expressions to program the computer to make a decision and act on it.

2.1 INTERNAL DATA MANIPULATION

Up to this point, it's been assumed that data would be used as received, whether it was hard coded into the program or entered by a user through a **getxxx** function. It's true that in the code used to draw the rectangle in Chapter 1, the X and Y coordinates of data points were interchanged, but the coordinates themselves were used as received. Now it's time to examine methods to massage the data, changing the given values.

Consider, for example, a program requiring a circle to be drawn one unit to the right and 2.325 units below a previously defined point. The center of the circle would have an X coordinate equal to the defined point's X coordinate plus one, and a Y coordinate 2.325 less than the point's Y coordinate. Taking the **car** and **cadr** of the given point gives us the X and Y coordinates, and adding (or subtracting) the required distances produces the required point. The coding below shows the complete operation:

```
(setq newpoint
   (list
       (+ (car p1) 1.0)
       (- (cadr p1) 2.325)
    )
)
```

Although the coding looks complex, it is simple to understand if you treat it the same way as a mathematical expression—by starting with the innermost parentheses, as shown in Figure 2.1. In this figure, the **car** and **cadr** terms are placed inside the parentheses labeled 1a and 1b. That gives us the X and Y coordinates. Parentheses 2a and 2b change the values of the old coordinates through addition or subtraction. Parentheses 3 enclose the **list** function, and put the newly created coordinates into the list form. The last parentheses set the value of *NEWPT* to the newly created list.

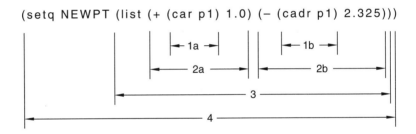

Parentheses	Function
1a (car p1)	Selects X coordinate of P1
1b (cadr p1)	Selects Y coordinate of P1
2a (+ 1.0)	Adds 1 to X coordinate of P1
2b (– 2.325)	Subtracts 2.325 from Y coordinate of P1
3 (list)	Creates a list of the new X and Y coordinates
4 (setq NEWPT)	Sets variable *NEWPT* to coordinates specified in the revised list

FIGURE 2.1   Nested Parentheses.

Although AutoLISP accepts the compound list shown above, it could be written like this, saving a great deal of space:

```
(setq newpoint (list (+ (car p1) 1.0)(- (cadr p1) 2.325))))
```

and would accomplish the same thing.

As their experience increases, AutoLISP programmers tend to put more than one function on a single line, but the expanded version is easier to understand and, if necessary, to correct.

AutoLISP can change the value of numerical data through the use of arithmetic operators (Table 2.1). These functions will accept either real or integer values. If all the inputs are integer, an integer is returned, but if one or more of the inputs are real, a real value will be returned. The data must be supplied as decimals (even if AutoCAD is set up for fractions), and in the case of real numbers, a digit must be both to the right and left of the decimal point. (In other words, 2.0, not 2., and 0.375, not .375). Whether real or integer, these functions return atoms, not lists.

TABLE 2.1   Arithmetic Operators

Function	Notes
(+ a b c . . .)	$a + b + c + \ldots$
(- a b c . . .)	$a - b - c - \ldots$
(* a b c . . .)	a times b times c times . . .
(/ a b c . . .)	a divided by b divided by c . . .
(1+ a)	$a + 1$
(1- a)	$a - 1$
(abs a)	Absolute (positive) value of a
(exp num)	Returns e raised to the *num* power
(expt num1 num2)	Returns *num1* to the *num2* power
(log num)	Returns natural log of *num*
(max num1 num2 . . .)	Returns maximum value
(min num1 num2 . . .)	Returns minimum value
(minusp item)	Returns T if item is number < 0
pi	A constant, not a function, evaluates to 3.141592 . . .
(rem num1 num2 . . .)	Returns remainder of *num1/num2/* . . .
(sqrt num)	Returns square root of *num*
(zeroop item)	Returns T if item evaluates to 0

2.2   LOGICAL OPERATORS

The operators discussed above *change* numerical values. There are also operators that *compare* both integer and string values; these are called logical operators. Logical operators are almost invariably associated with logical functions, discussed in the next section. The operators are used to form so-called **Test Expressions**, which, when evaluated, return a value of either T (for true) or nil (for false).

Soon you will be looking at the logical operator/logical function combination in action, but let's just get a feel for how logical operators are used. Suppose there is a situation where, if the horizontal distance between two points is greater than or equal to six, you have to do one thing, and if the distance is less than six, you have to do something else. A test expression can check whether the points are closer than six units apart, then a logical function can be used to act on the information. The **Test Expression** could look like this:

```
(<      ;less than operator
  (abs ;takes absolute value of following operation
  (- (car a) (car b));subtracts X coordinate of B from A
  6 ;test distance
);closes absolute function
);closes test expression
```

In this case, things might be clearer if the expression were written this way:

```
(< (abs (- (car a)(car b)) 6))
```

The absolute function is necessary because there is no way of knowing whether *A* or *B* has the greater X coordinate—if you subtract the larger from the smaller, you'll *always* end up with a value less than six. In setting up **Test Expressions**, always plan for the worst possible case. In this instance, you can program around the possible problem. If this proves to be impossible, consider another approach to solving the problem or set up prompts to lead the operator around the possible source of trouble.

In the example above, you essentially compared two numerical values, even though you had to get the distance by working with variables. As mentioned, logical operators may also be used to compare strings.

It may not seem odd to think of using a computer to compare 576 and 257, but is "apple" greater or less than "orange"? Think of comparing strings as a ranking operation instead of a numerical one. All computers represent the characters on your keyboard by numerical codes. Most computers use the ASCII (American Standard for Computer Information Interchange) code, which ranks the characters 0 through 9 ahead of the characters A through Z, which in turn are ahead of the characters a through z. This means that any string typed at the terminal can be compared to any other string on a character-to-character basis to determine which comes first (i.e., which one has a lower numerical value). Numbers are represented by a coding system that allows the number 27 to rank ahead of the number 100.

Logical operators allow the comparison of codes representing non-numerical values with each other, and the values of numerical values with each other. But they do not allow the comparison of the number 27 with the string "twenty two". These comparisons can only return two valid results: T (true) or nil (false), and it is up to the programmer to see that AutoLISP takes the appropriate action, depending on which of the two values are returned. The logical functions are summarized in Table 2.2.

Several of the logical functions appear to duplicate each other, but they don't. The **=**, **eq**, and **equal** functions comprise one such group. All three of them compare two items and return T if the items are "equal," but they attach different meanings to the word.

The **=** function comes closest to the normal use of the word equal. It compares two or more numbers or strings and returns T if they have the same numerical value or, in the case of strings, have identical ASCII codes.

TABLE 2.2   Logical Functions

Function	Notes
(= a b)	a equals b
(/= a b)	a is not equal to b
(< a b)	a is less than b
(<= a b)	a is less than or equal to b
(> a b)	a is greater than b
(>= a b)	a is greater than or equal to b
(eq a b)	a and b bound to the same object
(assoc item (assoc list). . .)	Returns **cadr** of assoc list sublist that starts with item
(equal a b fuzz)	a and b are within fuzz of each other
(and EXP1, EXP2 . . .)	T if all EXP are true
(foreach a lst exp)	Takes each item in *lst* and substitutes it for *a* in the expression
(minusp num)	T if *num* is negative real or integer
(not ITEM)	T if ITEM is nil
(null ITEM)	T if the value of ITEM is nil
(or EXP1 EXP2 . . .)	T if any EXP is true

On the other hand, **eq** returns T only if the items are bound to the same object. Consider the following coding:

```
(setq X 35
      AA X
      BB X
      CC AA
)
```

whereas (= AA CC), (= AA BB), or (**eq** AA BB) would all return T, (**eq** AA CC) would not, since CC is *not* bound to the same object as AA even though they both equate to the same value.

The **equal** function allows the user to specify how much two items can differ and still be "equal." This can be of critical importance, since two "equal" values determined by differing, but valid, mathematical approaches may not be "equal." Consider a 45-degree triangle with one-unit horizontal and vertical sides.

If Corner A is known, Corner B may be found by moving one unit over and one unit up from A, or by using the Pythagorean theorem to determine the direct distance from A to B (by taking the square root of the sum of the two sides), and moving that distance at a 45-degree angle. Both of these are valid approaches from a mathematical standpoint, and point B could be specified by AutoCAD using either approach. However, because of rounding errors, the computer's method of calculating square roots may differ from the true value in the last few decimal places. In addition, because AutoLISP uses radian measure for angles, a conversion factor (pi/180) must be used. But pi is not an exact number, so 45 degrees doesn't convert to its *exact* radian equivalent. Given AutoCAD's 15 decimal place precision, the errors can be ignored for practical purposes, but as far as the = function is concerned, a comparison of point B found by the one-over-one-up method with the one found using the square root of two will return nil. The optional third argument in the **equal** function serves as a fuzz factor, allowing the function to return a T when the items compared are equivalent for practical purposes.

You can check this out for yourself from the drawing editor. Enter the following code:

```
(setq A (list 0 0 0)
      B (list (1+ (car A))(1+ (cadr a)) 0)
)
```

Use UCS to rotate the coordinate system 45 degrees, then enter the following line:

```
(setq B1 (list (sqrt 2) 0 0))
```

If Pythagoras was right, points B and B1 should be the same. Indeed, if you enter "!B" and "!B1" from the command line, they will appear to have the same values. However, (= B B1) yields nil. On the other hand, (**equal** B B1 0.00001) returns T. Figure 2.2 illustrates the differences between the = and **equal** functions.

The logical functions **not** and **null** also appear to be duplicates at first glance. The former is used to return a T when a TEST expression evaluates to nil. For example, given (setq a 3 b 4), (= a b); returns nil, but (not (= a b)) returns T.

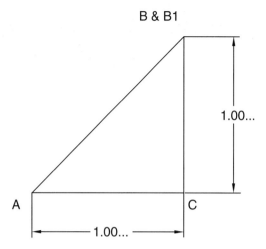

Notes:

Point B is found by drawing a one-unit long horizontal line from A,
then a one-unit long vertical line.

The length of line A–B1 is found by using the Pythagorean theorem
and drawing a line of that length at a 45-degree angle.

(= B B1) returns a value of nil.
(equal B B1 0.00001) returns a value of T.

FIGURE 2.2   Comparison of = and Equal Functions.

The **null** function returns T when an expression is bound to nil. This is a good test
for finding out if the expression has been correctly bound to a value.

Strictly speaking, **assoc** is not a logical function. It is included in this section
because it is generally used with the **if** or equivalent logical control functions discussed
in the next section.

Assoc is used with a special kind of list called an association list. An association list
comprises one or more two-atom sublists. The first atom in each of the sublists is treated as
a string. The association list behaves like a record in a data processing environment; that
is, it contains a variety of information pertaining to one specific entity which can be
extracted using the appropriate methods. For example, suppose you have employee information stored as shown at the top of the following page:

```
(setq a1 (("NAME" "Smith") ("GRADE" 5) ("PHONE" 123))
```

. . . additional lists . . .

```
   a100 (("NAME" "Jones") ("GRADE" 3) ("PHONE" 456))
);close setq
```

You could include the variables a1 . . . a100 in a list called *EMP*, and use the coding below to extract an individual's phone number.

```
         (foreach n emp
;goes through list of employees' association lists
          (if (= (assoc 'name n) "SMITH"))
;tests for list with sublist "NAME" "SMITH"
              (setq number (assoc "PHONE"))
;|if it is the list we want, the number associated with "PHONE" is
set to the variable "number" |;
          );closes if
        );goes to next list named in "emp"
```

The **foreach** function goes through the *EMP* list and substitutes each atom, in turn, for *N* in the **if** statment. When *N* is equal to "SMITH", the **if** is satisfied and assigns the value for PHONE on that line to the variable *NUMBER*, thus extracting Smith's phone number from the collected data.

Of course, AutoLISP is designed to act on drawing entities, not personnel files but, as will be seen later, **assoc** can be used to search through the drawing database for an entity with specific characteristics, in the same way it searched through the personnel list.

2.2.1   Using Logical Functions

Logical functions permit the computer to make decisions without operator intervention. Remember the rectangle-drawing example in Chapter 1? Suppose that the two pick points, P1 and P2, represent two devices that are to be connected with a vertical and a horizontal line with the longest line connected to the first point (P1). How can the computer decide how to draw the connections?

First, the horizontal and vertical distances are obtained by subtracting the **car** and the **cadr** of P1 from those of P2. Then the absolute values of the two distances are compared. If the X distance is greater than the Y distance then a horizontal line is drawn from P1; if not, a vertical line is drawn from P1. The line is drawn to an intermediate point (determined by the same procedure as used in the rectangle program), then to P2. Simple, isn't it?

At this point, one might ask, "What if both lines are the same length?" This is not a trivial question: you want the computer to make a choice, and if you don't anticipate all possibilities, the computer will be unable to make a decision under all the possible conditions.

The solution is quite simple in this case: set the program up so that if the distances are equal a horizontal line will be drawn.

The procedure outlined above will establish the logic needed to have the computer give the required output, but it doesn't answer the basic question of how to get the computer to make the decision. To accomplish this, we must allow the computer to control the order in which it accepts AutoLISP instructions. Table 2.3 summarizes the logical control functions that allow the computer to determine the order in which it accepts AutoLISP instructions.

Three of the functions use an explicit **Test** expression.[1] This expression may embody any of the logical functions discussed above. If the expression returns T the computer executes the **Then** statement, otherwise it goes to the optional **Else** statement or the next statement in the program. The **if** function (Figure 2.3) can execute only one **Then** statement (but it can be tricked—more about that later). The other functions can include multiple expressions within their **Then** statements. The **cond** function (Figure 2.4) allows multiple **Test** expressions to be evaluated, and acts on the first one that returns T. Think of **cond** as a multiple **if** function. It evaluates the first **Test**. If the first test statement is true, the program exits from the **cond** statement. If the first test statement isn't true, **cond** goes on to evaluate the next **Test**. This cycle is repeated until **Test** returns true.

Both the **while** function (Figure 2.5) and **repeat** function (Figure 2.6) will repeat groups of **Then** statements until either the **while Test** expression returns nil or the number of repetitions specified for the **repeat** statement has been met.

TABLE 2.3 Logical Control Functions

Function	Notes
(cond ((TEST (THEN)) ((TEST)(THEN)) . . .)	Goes through each TEST/THEN pair until T is returned, then exits from function
(if (TEST) (THEN) <ELSE>)	If TEST returns T, THEN is executed; if nil is returned, ELSE is executed
(prog (THEN) (THEN) . . .)	Allows multiple responses for THEN and ELSE in **if** function
(repeat num (THEN)(THEN) . . .)	Repeats the THENs *num* times
(while (TEST) (THEN) (THEN). . .)	Evaluates TEST until it is nil, then returns value of the last THEN

---

[1]The counter in the **repeat** function and the length of the list in the **foreach** function act as implicit **Test**s.

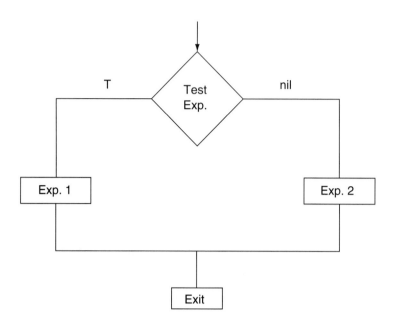

Example

```
(if                ;Open IF function
  (< A B)          ;Test expression
    (setq C A)     ;Action expression for "T"
    (setq C B)     ;Action expression for "nil"
)                  ;Close IF
```

FIGURE 2.3   The If Function.

By using these logical control functions, the computer can be programmed to make a decision and act on it. The coding below will draw a horizontal line from P1 to the intermediate point and then to P2 if the X distance is greater, and a vertical line if it is not.

```
    ;set DX to the X distance, DY to the Y distance
(setq dx (abs (- (car p2) (car p1)))
      dy (abs (- (cadr p2) (cadr p1)))
      intx (list (cadr p2)(car p1));point for horizontal line
      inty (list (car p1)(cadr p2));point for vertical line
);closes setq
(if (>= dx dy);test expression
        (command "LINE" p1 intx p2 "");if true do this
        (command "LINE" p1 inty p2 "");otherwise do this
);closes if
```

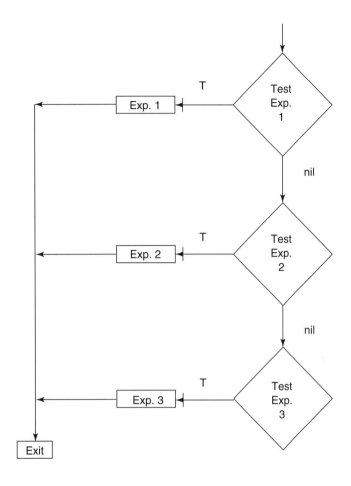

```
(cond                          ;Open function
  (( > A 0)                    ;1st test expression
    (setq TYPE "plus)          ;1st action expression
  )                            ;Close 1st test
  (( < A 0)                    ;2nd test expression
    (setq TYPE "minus)         ;2nd action expression
  )                            ;Close 2nd test
  (T (setq TYPE "zero"))       ;3rd test expression and
                               ;3rd action expression
)                              ;Close function
```

FIGURE 2.4   The Cond Function.

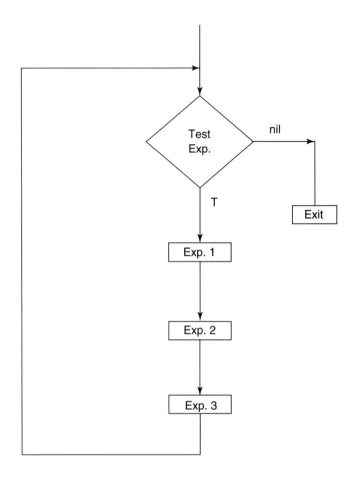

Example

```
(setq X 3)                  ;Set starting value
(while                      ;Open WHILE
  (< X 10)                  ;Test expression
   (setq X (+ 1 X)          ;Expression 1
         Y (+ (exp X 2) 7)  ;Expression 2
         pt (list X Y)      ;Expression 3
   )                        ;Close SETQ
   (command "POINT" pt)     ;Action expression
)                           ;Close WHILE
```

FIGURE 2.5   The While Function.

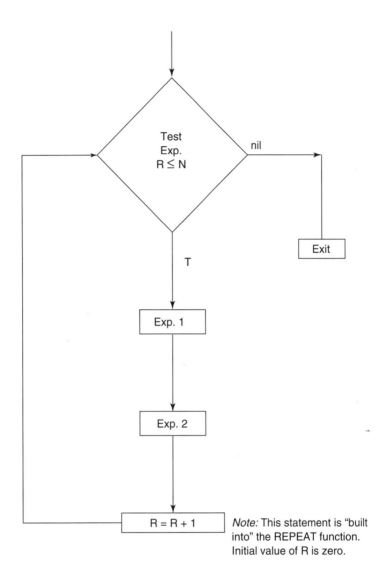

Note: This statement is "built into" the REPEAT function. Initial value of R is zero.

Example

(repeat 3	;Set N to 3 repetions
(setq A (* 5 A)	;Open SETQ, 1st expression
B (+ A B)	;Second expression
)	;Close SETQ
)	;Close REPEAT

FIGURE 2.6   The Repeat Function.

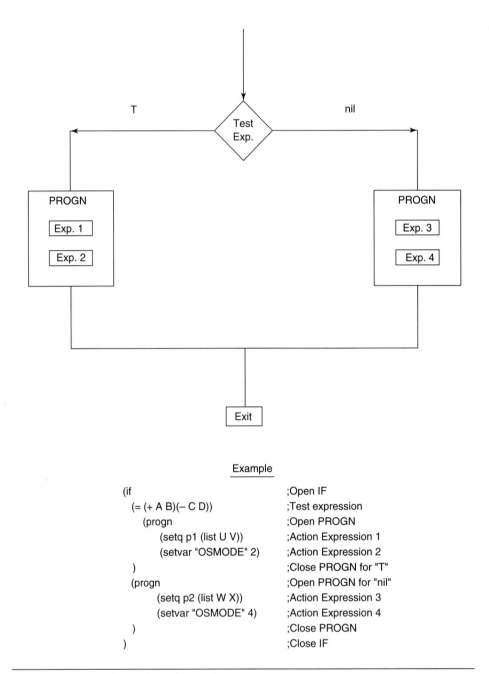

Example

```
(if                              ;Open IF
   (= (+ A B)(- C D))            ;Test expression
      (progn                     ;Open PROGN
          (setq p1 (list U V))   ;Action Expression 1
          (setvar "OSMODE" 2)    ;Action Expression 2
      )                          ;Close PROGN for "T"
   (progn                        ;Open PROGN for "nil"
          (setq p2 (list W X))   ;Action Expression 3
          (setvar "OSMODE" 4)    ;Action Expression 4
      )                          ;Close PROGN
   )                             ;Close IF
```

FIGURE 2.7   The If (with Progn) Function.

As mentioned above, the **if** function can take only one **Then** statement, but by using the **progn** function (Figure 2.7), this limitation may be circumvented. Suppose, for example, you wanted to have the horizontal line created on layer HOR, and the vertical line on layer VER. Compare the coding below for an **if** using the **progn** function, with the previous method of connecting P1 to P2.

```
(if (>= dx dy)
    (progn
      (setq intm (list (cadr p2)(car p1)))
      (command "LAYER" "S" "HOR" "")
    );closes progn
    (progn
        (setq intm (list (car p1)(cadr p2)))
        (command "LAYER" "S" VER" "")
    );closes progn
);closes if
(command "LINE" p1 intm p2 "")
```

Notice how the **if** function was only used to set up the conditions for drawing the line. The actual drawing was done after **if** was closed. This is a more efficient program than it would be if a **command** function was included in each of the **progn** functions since it saves typing at least one line of code. When working with logical functions, try to set them up so that any operations that are common to all the alternatives are done outside, rather than within, the control loop.

EXERCISES

The main purpose of these exercises is to give you practice in developing AutoLISP programs to solve problems. Assume that the necessary variables have been entered in the proper form. Once you've solved the basic problem, it is a relatively simple matter to program input to the required variables.

1. The quadratic equation, beloved of algebra teachers, tells us that the positive root of a quadratic can be found using the relationship:

$$r = \frac{-b + \sqrt{(b^2 - 4ac)}}{2a}$$

Write an AutoLISP expression that will calculate the root of the equation $ax^2 + bx + c = 0$ and assign it to the variable *ROOT*.

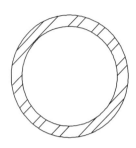

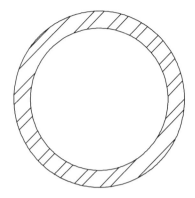

Flow < 7 gpm   Flow ≥ 7 gpm

FIGURE 2.8

2. The cross-sectional area of a certain pipe is determined by the flow through it (see Figure 2.8). If the flow is equal to or greater than 7 gal/min, the diameter is to be 1.25 inches. If the flow is less than that, the diameter need only be 0.875 inches. Write the code that will correctly size the variable *DIA,* depending on the value of *FLOW*.

3. Write the code that will get the seventh power of the value of the variable *TEST* by multiplying *TEST* by itself six times. Make the code such that if we decide to raise *TEST* to the tenth power, it can be done by changing only one line of code.

4. A factorial number is the product of a number times all the positive nonzero integers less than the given number. For example factorial 3, written 3!, is 3 * 2 * 1 = 6. (For the record, 0! is defined as being equal to 1.) Write the code to determine the value of the largest number whose factorial is less than 1250.

5. A certain program establishes points based on the value of the variable *DIR*. If *DIR* = "N", the variable *PT* is set to the list (0 1). If *DIR* is "W", "S", or "E", *PT* is to be set to the lists (–1 0), (0 –1), and (1 0), respectively. Write the code that will properly set *PT*.

CHAPTER 3

User-Defined Functions, Shortcuts, and Conversions

OBJECTIVES

After reading this chapter, you should be able to:

- String AutoLISP functions together to form a user-defined function (UDF).

- Use AutoLISP's distance, angle, and intersection functions to locate points without additional user input.

- Convert distances and angles in string format to numerical format and vice versa.

3.1 AUTOLISP PROGRAMMING SHORTCUTS

One of the greatest timesavers available to AutoLISP programmers is the capability of stringing AutoLISP functions together to form a user-defined function (UDF). A UDF or program is a simple or compound list containing predefined AutoLISP functions and, optionally, data. A program must start off with an AutoLISP **defun** statement. **Defun** is the AutoLISP function that creates functions and, like all AutoLISP functions, it must be placed between parentheses. In the case of **defun**, its leading parenthesis constitutes the start of the program and the end parenthesis terminates the program.

Information is supplied to user-defined functions in a number of ways:

Arguments, or global variables, are variables that have been defined outside the UDF. Their values may be changed *within* the function but upon exiting the

UDF, globals revert to their former values.[1] Globals' values must be supplied to the UDF when it is called upon, so, for example, UDF **xyz** with two arguments would be invoked by coding:

```
(xyz G1 G2)
```

in the main program.

Local variables are defined and used within the UDF; they are not available for use outside the program. The memory space that AutoLISP uses to store the values of local variables is released when the UDF is terminated.

Undeclared variables are external variables that can be revalued within the program and will retain the new values when the UDF is concluded. Since they are not declared in the UDF's **defun** statement, undeclared variables cannot be called up by calling the function but must be supplied by external statements.

Now run through a series of simple UDFs, to illustrate the characteristics of local and global variables. Consider the coding below:

```
(setq a 2)
(defun TEST ()
    (setq a (* 2 a)
          b 15)
)
```

If you type this in at the command line, when you hit the enter key, the computer will print out **test**, the last function evaluated.

Since *A* is an undeclared variable, its value can be changed. It's 2 going in to the function. If you call the function by typing "(test)" at the command line, the computer will return 15, the value of the last function evaluated. However, if you enter !a (or !A) at the command prompt, you'll see that the value for *A* is 4, not 2! That's because *A* is an undeclared variable, and its value is subject to change.

Notice the required parentheses following the name of the function—that's where the arguments and local symbols go. We'll see them in action later. The parentheses *must* follow the name of the function (which is case insensitive).

Now, let's try another variation. Set *B* to a value and declare it as a local variable by entering it inside the parentheses with a slash and a space preceeding it:[2]

---

[1] Don't be confused by the fact that many UDFs accept a global variable that appears to have changed its value without ever having been redefined by a **setq**. The change did not occur *inside* the UDF (see **Test3**) but rather after exiting the function. The value of the global was redefined by **setq**ing it to the value returned by the UDF (see **Test4**).

[2] The argument list for **defun** is one of the few places where AutoLISP is restrictive about format. If a function has no arguments or local symbols, a space and a pair of parentheses (with or without a space) must immediately follow **defun**. AutoLISP uses a slash (/) inside these parentheses to separate arguments and local symbols. If the slash is present, there must be at least one space between the arguments in front of it and the slash, and between the slash and the local symbols behind it. This means that (), (A B), (/ C D), and (A / B C) are acceptable, but (A/B C) isn't.

```
  (setq b 21)
(defun TEST2 (/ b)
    (setq b 44)
)
```

Again, when the function is called between parentheses, the computer returns the value of the last function evaluated; in this case 44. The variable *B* was set to 44 in the UDF, but since it was a local, the new value was not available outside the function. Thus, when you enter !b, 21 is returned, not 44.

Now let's try to combine global and local values. Both types go in the parentheses that follow the function name, the global variable or variables ahead of the slash, and the locals after it. Put a space on each side of the slash.

```
(defun TEST3 (a / b)
    (setq a 10 b 3 c (* b a) d 1)
)
```

Since TEST3 uses a global symbol (they're usually called arguments, to distinguish them from the purely local symbols), it must get a value to use in place of *A* inside the function. The value must be consistent with the argument inside the function. That is, if an argument represents a string in a given function, a string must be supplied when the function is called up. The value may be supplied as a string, a number, or a variable representing a string or a number. The name of the variable doesn't have to be the same as the name in the function's argument list, but the quantity it represents must be the proper type for the UDF to operate on. In this case, let's assign a numerical value to a variable.

```
(setq xyz 4)
(test3 xyz)
```

The function returns 1, the last value, but !xyz returns 4, not 10, since *XYZ*, a global, was previously set to 4 and retains its value upon exiting the UDF. What about *C*? It's an external variable so it can be redefined inside the function. Will its value be $3 \times 10 = 30$ (with *XYZ* set to 10) or $3 \times 4 = 12$ (with *XYZ* set to 4)? Entering !C returns 30, because even though *XYZ* must leave the function set to its entering value, nothing stops the function from changing *XYZ*'s value and using the changed value *inside* the function.

In the function above, *A* was used to represent a variable in the definition of **test3** and *XYZ* to represent a variable that was fed to the function in *A*'s place. As mentioned above, it isn't necessary that they both be the same: any legal variable can stand in for a variable of the same type. But using the same variable in the function and to test the function does help the programmer in two ways. First, by defining the variable just before feeding it to the function, the programmer will know what values are being used inside the function. Second, using the name of the test variable in writing the **defun** statement for the function makes the function's logic clearer. So when you're writing a function, it makes sense to use the same global variable names both outside and inside the function. Once the function is operational, there's no reason to stick to this convention.

The **test3** function showed that you can't change the value of a global inside the function, but it is still possible to use a function to redefine a global. The trick is to use the function to redefine the variable *outside* the function. For example, consider the function below:

```
(defun TEST4 (v)
    (setq v (+ 1 v))
)
```

Now, look at this coding:

```
(setq v 24)
(TEST4 v)
```

You already looked at this situation when you tried **test3**. The function redefines *V* internally and, upon exiting, resets *V* to its global value (24) and returns the value of the last function evaluated, in this case 25. Now what will happen if you change the coding, as shown below?

```
(setq v 24)
(setq v (TEST4 v))
```

Test4 would return 25 *inside* the second **setq** but *outside* the function, **setq** sets the value of *V* to the returned value. Everything is legal, but the end result is that **test4** redefined *V* as a global!

Functions **test1** through **test4** all had to be entered between parentheses at the command line. UDFs may also be entered *without* parentheses if the function's name in the **defun** statement is prefaced by "C:" or "c:". To all intents and purposes, this option permits the UDF to be treated as an AutoCAD command. If it doesn't use the **command** function or cause a **regen,** the C-named UDF can be used transparently. AutoCAD commands can also be used transparently from within the UDF, and, should you misspell the name of the UDF, AutoCAD will return the familiar "Unknown command. Type ? for list of commands" prompt. However, C-named UDFs come with a price: they cannot call global variables (local and undeclared variables are permitted). C-named functions are useful both for simple programs (particularly if you keep their names short) as well as for complex programs that call on other UDFs. In a later chapter you will learn how to use a UDF to call up a number of simple UDFs to accomplish a complex task.

3.2 COMPUTATIONAL SHORTCUTS

In drawing a rectangle, AutoLISP gave points to the AutoCAD drawing editor, which, in turn, used the information derived from the points to draw the box. The process can work the other way too. Given the location of points on a drawing, AutoLISP can calculate the distances and angles between them, determine the location of the intersection of lines connecting the points, and even use the existing points to supply information for establishing new points. You saw this capability in Chapter 2 when the user picked the points used to derive the coordinates of the other corners of the box. Then, the information was derived by separating the X and Y coordinates using **car** and **cadr**. Now let's learn about a more direct method.

All AutoLISP functions dealing with angles expect input to be in radians. Since most people tend to think in terms of degrees, this presents something of a problem. Fortunately, AutoLISP supplies the constant **pi** that can be used in converting angles to radians (or radians to angles, for output). The two coded segments below should be included with any program involving manipulation of angles. The **dtr** function converts from *degrees* to *radians*.

```
(defun dtr (a)
   (setq a (* a (/ pi 180)))
)

;|since A is externally supplied to the function, the function
cannot be prefaced by C: |;

(defun RTD (a)
    (setq a (* a (/ 180 pi)))
)
```

The **polar** function may be used (together with some elementary right-angle trigonometry) to simplify some constructions. Consider, for example, the problem of locating a point (P2) at a known angle (*ANG*) and distance (*DIST*) from a picked point (P1). Using the **car** and **cadr** of the initial point, distance, and the sine and cosine of the angle, the second point could be located by coding similar to this:

```
(setq x (cdr p1);x coordinate of p1
      y (cadr p1);y coordinate
      dx (* dist (sin ang));x distance
      dy (* dist (cos ang));y distance
      p2 (list (- x dx) (+ y dy));coordinate list
)
```

Using the **polar** function, the same objective could be reached by:

```
(set p2 (polar p1 ang dist))
```

Using **polar** also eliminates the problem of dealing with the changing positive or negative values of **sin** and **cos** in the different quadrants.

Even though it might be useful, there is no AutoLISP function to directly determine the tangent of an angle. Since the tangent of an angle involves dividing the opposite side of a triangle by the adjacent side, the absolute value of the tangent becomes infinite when the adjacent side is equal to zero. Computers can handle big numbers, but not the value of infinity. Therefore, a program using a tangent function to calculate the tangent of 90 or 270 degrees ($\pi/2$ or $3*\pi/2$ radians) would fail. Of course, if the tangent of an angle were needed, it could be calculated, but the program would have to be protected against an inadvertent instruction to calculate a value for infinity. One approach is:

```
(setq a (sin ang)
      b (cos ang)
)
(if (/= b 0)  ;if the cosine isn't 0
  (setq tan (/ a b))  ;calculate Tan
      (setq tan "DIVISION BY ZERO")
          ;else give an error message
  )
```

Of course, when *TAN* is used in a situation calling for a numerical value, the program will crash. In this case, a crash is the best thing to hope for, since there must be a flaw in the fundamental logic behind the program. This way, when the programmer starts to debug the program by getting the value for the variable *TAN* (for instance, by entering "!tan" from the command line), the message will give an indication of the cause of failure.

The **atan** function is the only one available for relating the slope of a line to its angle. If a single positive argument is supplied, the angle returned will be between 0 and $\pi/2$ radians. If the argument is negative, a negative angle will be returned. If two arguments are supplied, the angle will fall between the values indicated below.

a	b	Radians	Degrees
1	1	.7854 . . .	45
1	−1	2.3561 . . .	135
−1	1	−0.7854 . . .	−45
1	−1	−2.3561 . . .	−135
1	0	1.5708 . . .	90
0	1	0	0
−1	0	−1.5708 . . .	−90
0	−1	3.1415 . . .	360

Angles in the first and second quadrant are returned directly as radians; those in the third and fourth quadrants are returned as negative (clockwise) angles. If necessary, an **if** statement can be added at the end of the codes for both **dtr** and **rtd** to ensure the return of a positive value. For **rtd** the additional coding should resemble:

```
    (defun rtd (a) ...
1       (if (> 0 a)
2         (setq a (+ 360 a))
```

```
3          )
     );close defun
```

Line 2 should be replaced by (setq a (+ (* pi 2) a) for **dtr**.

There are trigonometric relationships that will allow the calculation of inverse sines and cosines, given the appropriate arctangent, but they are complicated and lead to complex multi-nested expressions. In the event that arcsine or arccosine are needed, use the Pythagorean theorem to calculate the missing side by taking the square root of one minus the square of the sine (or cosine) squared, then supplying the value of the two sides to **atan**. If both **sin** and **cos** are available, the value of the angle may be found by dividing **sin** by **cos** and submitting the result to **atan**. Distance, angle, and intersection functions are summarized in Table 3.1.

3.3   CHANGING DATA TYPES

When external data is supplied to AutoCAD (for example, in response to a request for a circle's radius) or to a prompt requesting a layer's name, any rational response will be accepted. The program is powerful enough to convert an integer radius to a real number,

TABLE 3.1   Distance, Angle, and Intersection Functions

Function	Notes
(angle pt1 pt2)	Returns the angle (in radians) made by the line from Pt1 to Pt2 and the positive X axis
(distance pt1 pt2)	2-D or 3-D distance between Pt1 and Pt2
(inters pt1 pt2 pt 3 pt 4 [char])	Returns the 2-D or 3-D coordinates of the intersection of the line formed by Pt1 and Pt2 with line Pt3, Pt4. If the optional *char* is present and nil, the lines are considered infinite; otherwise they are finite and the intersection must lie between the endpoints of both lines
(atan num [num2])	Returns arctangent in radians
(cos ang)	Returns cosine of radian angle
(osnap pt modes)	Returns point found by applying OSNAP mode(s) to Pt
(polar pt ang dist)	Returns the coordinates of a point *dist* away from Pt at radian angle of *ang*
(sin ang)	Returns sine of radian angle

or a numeric name for a block to a string. This capability extends, to a lesser extent, to information supplied to AutoLISP's **command** function. Inside AutoLISP itself, though, the situation is not as clear-cut. Numerical information may be supplied as real or integer numbers, but strings must be in quotes.

AutoLISP data comes in various types and in many forms: integers, strings, real numbers (with varying numbers of decimal places), and several varieties of angular measurement. If the data is entered through a **getXXX** function, it may be automatically configured to the appropriate type. For example, entering 2.0 in response to a **getstring** prompt will return the string "2.0." However, if 2.02 were entered at a **getint** prompt, the computer would return an error message. Of course, a string entry in response to **getint** or **getreal** would not be accepted.

Once the data has been assigned to an AutoLISP variable, it may be used for many purposes. At times, the data may not be in the proper form or of the proper type for a given AutoLISP function to accept it. One example of this type of situation is when blocks or text styles are assigned numerical names so that they can be referenced sequentially. Blocks and styles must have strings for names, yet to reference them sequentially, one must have numerical values. A similar problem arises when a string must be combined with a real or integer number. AutoLISP has a function that will concatenate (combine) strings, but not one that will combine strings and nonstrings. Here, the numbers must be converted to strings.

In a later chapter, you'll see that any data read into a program from an external file must be in the form of a string. If this data represents numerical values, it must be converted into integers or reals for use in AutoLISP.

TABLE 3.2   Data Type Conversion Functions

Function	Notes
(angtof string [mode])*	String to real number in UNITS command mode
(angtos angle [mode] [precision])*	Real number in radians to string in UNITS command format and specified precision
(atof string)	String to real
(atoi string)	String to integer
(fix number)	Number to integer
(float number)	Number to real
(itoa integer)	Integer to string
(rtos real [mode][precision])[†]	Real to string

* If optional mode and precision are omitted, conversion will follow current settings of AUNITS and AUPREC system variables.

[†] If optional mode and precision are omitted, conversion will follow current settings of LUNITS and LUPREC system variables.

These problems can be worked out, but at the expense of either additional programming or changing the overall procedure. To avoid the necessity of the extra work, and to provide the user with the maximum flexibility, AutoLISP has a library of conversion functions to convert from one type of data to another.

Converting between real and integer values is relatively straightforward. In going from real to integer, decimal values are discarded. In the reverse direction, the real number is expressed with a specified number of zeros after the decimal point.[3] When strings are involved, though, the problem becomes more complex. Converting 2.356 . . . radians to "N45d'0.000W" or 25.5 to 2'1.5" is not a simple process, even for a computer! Table 3.2 shows the functions used to convert between integers, strings, and reals.

The optional "mode" term has a different meaning for the **angtof**, **angtos**, and **rtos** functions. In **angtos** (*angle to string*) and **angtof**, it may have an integer value of from 1 to 5, with the meanings shown in Table 3.3. The mode values in the **rtos** (*real to string*) function configure the output string to match the choices in AutoCAD's UNITS command. They are shown in Table 3.4. Table 3.5 will clarify the interrelationship between these functions.

TABLE 3.3 Angle to String (Angtos) Formats

Angtos Mode	Output Format
1	Degrees (e.g., 60.0000°)
2	Degrees/Min./Sec. (e.g., 60°0'0″)
3	Grads (e.g., 66.6667g)
4	Radians (e.g., 1.0471 rad)
5	Surveyor's Units (e.g., N 30° E)

TABLE 3.4 Real to String (Rtos) Formats

Rtos Mode	Output Format
1	Scientific (1.75E + 01)
2	Decimal (17.75)
3	Engineering (1' 5.75")
4	Architectural (1' 5¾")
5	Fractional (17¾)

---

[3]Since AutoCAD stores all real numbers with a 14- or 15-place accuracy, the question of false precision does not arise.

TABLE 3.5 Conversion Functions' Applications

		From		
To	Integer	Real	Real (Angle)	String
Angle				Angtof
Integer		Fix		Atoi
Real	Float			Atof
String	Itoa	Rtos	Angtos	

EXERCISES

Remember to concentrate on solving the core problem. Once you've done that, try your hand with writing the code for inputting the data. Don't forget the prompts—they should guide a user who isn't acquainted with the program through the input process. The code for the core problem is satisfactory if it does what it is supposed to do, and that's an easy matter to check. On the other hand, the ideal test for input prompts would be to grab someone off the street and have them run the program without any additional prompting from you. That kind of test isn't too easy to set up!

1. Write a UDF to accept values in inches and return millimeters if the input is less than 0.0394, centimeters if the input is between .0394 and 39.37, and meters if the input is greater than 39.37 (25.4 mm = 2.54 cm = .0254 m = 1 inch). The program is also to contain the variable *UNIT* which will be assigned a value of "mm," "cm," or "m," as appropriate.

2. Given a line from P1 to P2, write a code to draw the line from P3 to P4 where P3 is the midpoint of P1–P2, angle P1–P3–P4 is 90 degrees less than angle P1–P2, and the distance between P3 and P4 has been supplied by the operator.

3. The default for a command is assigned to the variable *DEF* as a string. Write the AutoLISP coding so that if the user strikes return as a response to the command, prompt *DEF* will be assigned to the variable *VAL* but if a numerical value is entered at the prompt, *VAL* will be set to that value.

4. Write the code for a UDF that would accept *A*, *B*, and *C* as arguments or symbols and use **list** or **quote** to make a list containing the strings assigned to the variables. Test your coding by using **setq** to assign string values to the variables. Try supplying only two values to the UDF. Can you find a way to omit string variables for a UDF and still have it work?

CHAPTER 4

Practical Programming I

OBJECTIVES

After reading this chapter, you will be able to:

- Write a program to clean up intersecting walls.
- Work with multiple offsets.
- Understand the uses of automatic linear dimensioning.
- Break any long program into six standard modules.

4.1   PRELIMINARY STEPS IN PROGRAMMING

At this point, you have enough tools to consider writing some real programs, but before you start programming, some questions need to be answered.

The first one, of course, is:

What do we want the program to do?

The programs you can write at this point fall into several classes.

1. Programs to replicate a string of AutoCAD commands.
2. Programs to speed up repetitive commands.
3. Programs to "improve" AutoCAD commands.

As an example of the first type of program, you will examine a program that allows the user to "clean up" junctions of walls formed by parallel lines. A program that uses OFFSET to set up a series of parallel lines at specified distances will serve as an example of the second type of program, and a program that lets the computer determine whether a line to be dimensioned requires a HORIZONTAL, VERTICAL, or ALIGNED dimension represents the third type of program.

The programs also serve to review the functions covered so far. The first program uses the **getpoint** and **command** functions and constructs points using **car** and **cadr**. The second program uses logic functions and lists. The third program illustrates the derivation of data points.

As it happens, the clean-up and dimensioning programs have been embodied in AutoCAD V.12 and 13 respectively, but at the time they were written (in the distant days of V.9), they offered a definite improvement over what was then directly available in as-received AutoCAD. Which brings up the second question:

Is the proposed program worth the effort to write it?

The answer to this question is subjective, and it depends on the individual doing the program, the savings in time or effort resulting from the program, and the tolerance of the programmer's supervisor. This issue is critical in the work place. No employer is willing to pay for programming if its direct and indirect costs are not offset by savings in drawing time or effort. This means you must be prepared to justify any time you spend on programming in terms of savings. If you learn programming on your own or in school, you'll be able to produce programs efficiently, reducing the amount of justification needed.

Beginning AutoCAD students probably haven't learned enough about AutoCAD's basic commands to use them in AutoLISP programs. Advanced AutoCAD students, on the other hand, will probably gain deeper insights into the computerized drafting process by integrating AutoCAD and AutoLISP programming and drafting techniques. *Doing* programming and studying others' programs is an excellent way to learn programming. It would be to your advantage to write all the programs you can.

The third question is:

How is the program going to work?

Here, it is not so important that you know how the commands work, but rather that you understand the method of attack to use in your program.

The clean-up program basically strings together a group of AutoLISP commands, essentially replicating the procedure that would be followed in the absence of a program: the commands are used in the same sequence as an operator would use them. The demands on the programmer are minimal, essentially requiring the selection of a number of points, then calling up a series of AutoCAD commands. Even if the program exactly duplicates an operator's procedure, it is still faster than the operator, because the commands are supplied electronically rather than through relatively slow human input.

The offset program is a step up in complexity. It sets up a list of offset distances, then supplies the list to the OFFSET command. It also involves the use of a logic function to control the content of the list.

The third program is the most complex of the three. In this program, a logic function controls command option selectivity, and geometric functions are employed to automatically establish data points based on a user-picked point.

These programs are not presented as outstanding examples of the programmers' art: there are probably more efficient AutoCAD commands to use, and more efficient methods of programming. However, they do accomplish the jobs they were designed to do using only commands you are already acquainted with. They save the user's time and make it easier to make drawings, and as such, they are worthy of study. As you go through them, notice how they attack the problem. See if you can accomplish their ends in a different manner and—perhaps most importantly—see whether you can apply the techniques in these programs to problems *you* face.

4.1.1 Cleaning Up Intersecting Walls

One way to represent walls of a building in architectural drawing is to draw a line to represent the outside of a wall, then use OFFSET to produce a parallel line at a distance of six or eight inches. This method is faster than drawing both sides of the wall, but it leaves intersecting offset lines wherever the exterior line changes direction. These lines can be removed by doing a ZOOM on the intersection, then using BREAK or TRIM to get rid of the excess portions of the interior lines. This usually involves the following steps:

1. ZOOM, Window (with two screen picks) from a large scale view to select the intersection area.
2. Select the interior intersection and a point beyond the end of the line (two or three picks per line to be removed) if BREAK is used, or the cutting planes and lines to be trimmed if TRIM is selected (two picks per line).
3. Do a ZOOM, Previous to get back to the overview, preparatory to selecting the next intersection.

In the worst case (where four walls meet), this requires two picks for the window, eight or twelve picks for the lines, and three command selections (ZOOM W, BREAK/TRIM, ZOOM P) as well as four INT osnaps if BREAK is used.

The AutoLISP approach relies on the fact that since walls are typically six or eight inches thick, the intersection will clearly show up on a screen that's 24 inches high. Once the intersection is visible, all entities in it can be selected for the TRIM command by using a Crossing Box for selection, then the lines to be trimmed can be selected by the user. To make picking easier, OSNAP will be set to Nearest for trimming.

A ZOOM, Window could be used to close in on the intersection, but that would require two picks. Is there a better way? A look at ZOOM in AutoCAD's HELP command discloses that there's a Center option for ZOOM. With this option, the user selects a point at or near the intersection and, using ZOOM's Center option with a 24-inch height, can ensure that the intersection appears in the window. After some consideration, it was decided to use an OSNAP, Intersection at the initial pick, and to instruct the user to select a point P1, at the lower-left-hand side of the intersection. This would ensure getting the intersection proper near the center of the screen.

In this program, the TRIM command was selected instead of BREAK because it requires fewer picks. Cutting planes can be selected with a Crossing Box (unlike BREAK), so, in the worst case, once the intersection is selected, only six additional picks are needed. Four lines can be trimmed by two picks (for the Crossing Box) and one pick on each of the four lines to be trimmed. Figure 4.1 shows the seven picks that need to be made to clean up the offset lines.

Specifying a 24-inch height for the screen means that the width will be about 32 inches. Thanks to the use of OSNAP, Intersection and ZOOM, Center, the lower-left corner of the intersection should be somewhere near the center of the screen, 12 inches from the top and bottom of the screen, and 16 inches from the sides. This gives you the envelope to work in.

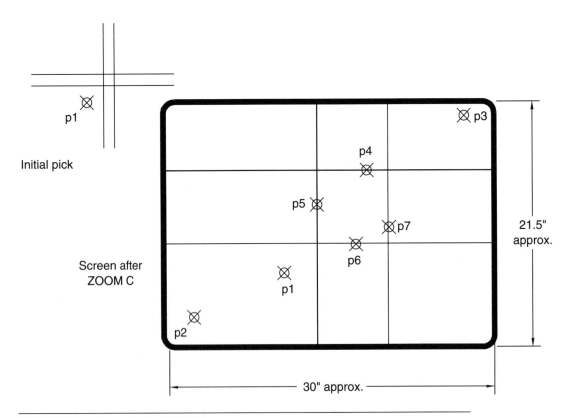

FIGURE 4.1   Geometry for CLEAN program.

The Crossing Box for picking the cutting planes can be set by moving 15 inches to the side and 10 inches above or below the initial pick point. The program will be set up for the worst-case scenario—four picks. Using OSNAP, Nearest to make picking easier, the program will prompt the user to make four picks on the lines to be trimmed. If only two or three picks are necessary, the user will be prompted to make null picks for the extra points.

If the program is to work properly, you must give some thought to the current state of the screen environment. For example, if SNAP is on with a large value, it may be difficult to move the cross hairs when zoomed in on the intersection. Therefore, you should be sure that SNAP is turned off while you're looking at the intersection. When you are finished, return SNAP to its initial setting; otherwise the user might lose the time gained with the program in resetting SNAP. The same is true in the case of OSNAP. The program first sets OSNAP to Intersection, then to Nearest, and the user who has OSNAP set to Midpoint might be in for an unpleasant surprise upon exiting from the program. The best way to handle these environmental issues is to save the values of the system variables or environmental commands you intend to use in your programs, assign the variables the values needed, then reset them to their old values before exiting. Using **getvar** to obtain the initial variable values and **setvar** for setting and resetting them is quicker than using **command** and OSNAP or SNAP to do the job. Of course, to use this approach, one must know the names of the appropriate system variables, in this case, OSMODE for OSNAP, and SNAPMODE for SNAP.[1]

Program 4.1 is the complete CLEAN program. Study it until you are sure that you understand how it functions. See if you can come up with alternate ways to ZOOM in on the intersection and get rid of the unnecessary lines. Are there any other environmental conditions that could cause troubles? Properly speaking, these questions should be asked and answered before—rather than after—coding, but since this is your first AutoLISP program, let's make an exception.

4.1.2   Multiple Offsets

When doing a drawing that uses ordinate dimensioning (i.e., a drawing with all dimensions taken from the lower-left corner of each view), or a drawing with only one orthographic view, it is a good idea to set up a construction layer and use the OFFSET command to establish critical centers and intersections. Once these points have been established, you can switch to the object layer, set OSNAP to Intersection, and "trace" most of the object lines. This is a fast, accurate way to do the job—much better than entering relative distances from the keyboard. Figure 4.2 shows how the XOFF programs can be used to draw multiple

---

[1]Most of the system variables are toggles that use 0 for the off state and 1 for on. Some, such as OSMODE, are multivalued. If you don't have a reference available, you can get the value for the state you need by using the appropriate command to set the value in the drawing editor, then entering the name of the variable at the command line. The current numerical value will be returned as a default.

PROGRAM 4.1—CLEANING UP WALLS (CLEAN)

```
;|              IMPORTANT!
Do not put blank lines in front of or inside LISP programs unless
they are included as comments. The comment symbols are the semicolon
(;) and the line/semicolon combination (;|), Use a semicolon-line for
opening a comment, and a line-semicolon to close it. This is where
you explain what the program does and how it does it. This program
cleans up the intersection of four parallel lines
representing six- or eight-inch thick walls.
                      Variables List
*************************************************************************
os, sn       Current values of OSMODE and SNAPMODE variables
msg1-msg3    Prompts
p1           Point to left of and below intersection
p2, p3       Diagonal points of 30 x 20 crossing box with p1 at the
             center
p4-p7        Lines to be trimmed or null picks for < 4 walls
*************************************************************************
|;
(defun C:CLEAN
            (/ os sn msg1 msg2 msg3 p1 p2 p3 p4 p5 p6 p7)
    (setq os (getvar "OSMODE")       ;get current OSNAP
          sn (getvar "SNAPMODE")     ;SNAP on/off
    )
    (setvar "OSMODE" 32)     ;set OSNAP to INTersection
    (setvar "SNAPMODE" 0)    ;turns off SNAP
    (setq msg1 "\nPick LL corner of intersection:"
          msg2 "\Pick line to be trimmed:   "
          msg3 "\nPick line to be trimmed or null:   "
            p1 (getpoint msg1)
            p2 (list
                  (- (car p1) 15) (- (cadr p1) 10)
;establishes point for lower-left corner of crossing box
                ) ;closes list for first corner
            p3 (list
                  (+ (car p1) 15) (+ (cadr p1) 10)
;|    p2 and p3 establish 30 x 20 crossing box to
      select walls forming intersection|;
                ) ;closes second list
);closes setq
    (command "ZOOM" "C" p1 24);ZOOM, Center at p1, 24 high
    (setvar "OSMODE" 512);OSNAP set to Nearest
    (setq p4 (getpoint msg2);sets point for
          p5 (getpoint msg2);selection of up to
          p6 (getpoint msg3);four walls to be
          p7 (getpoint msg3);trimmed
    )
    (command "TRIM" "C" p2 p3 "" p4 p5 p6 p7 ""
            "ZOOM" "P";returns to initial view
    )
    (setvar "OSMODE" os);returns to initial OSNAP
    (setvar "SNAPMODE" sn);returns to old SNAP status
);closes defun
```

offsets, which then establish the intersections used to define the major features of a view of an object.

The one drawback to this approach is the necessity of exiting, then re-entering the OFFSET command every time the offset distance has to be changed. Program 4.2 enables the user to offset single-line multiple distances with a single command.

The program begins by prompting the user to enter the first offset distance (which is entered into a list), select the object to be offset, and indicate the side to offset. The program then enters a loop, where it prompts the user for each of the other distances. Each of the distances is added in turn to the front of the list using **cons**. When the list is completed, the **foreach** function is used to apply the OFFSET command to each atom in the list.

Initially, the only problem with the program was the selection of the logical control function to terminate the distance entry portion of the program. One possibility was to request that the user preset the number of distances to be entered. The number would be used in a **repeat** loop which would terminate when the required number of values were entered. This approach was rejected, because it cut down on the program's flexibility—a miscount would require additional user commands. It was decided, instead, to use a "flag." Flags are signals used in data processing to indicate that some action is required from the computer. In this case, since AutoCAD will not accept zero as an offset distance, it was decided to use zero to tell the computer to terminate the distance entries. The user is prompted to "Enter a distance, or 0 to end:". When the zero is entered, the program moves on to the next phase.

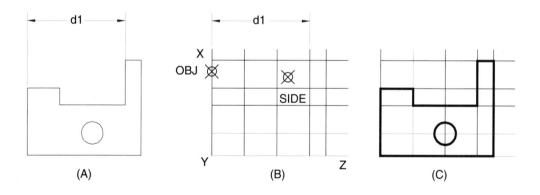

(A)   (B)   (C)

(A) View to be drawn with a typical horizontal distance shown.

(B) Completed grid drawn by using XOFF to offset lines XY and YZ.
     Notice how the line at d1 was produced by offsetting AB using points OBJ and SIDE and distance d1.

(C) View drawn (using a wide PLINE for contrast) by setting OSNAP to INTersection and picking the
     appropriate intersections of the grid for the endpoints of the lines and the center of the circle.

FIGURE 4.2   Application of XOFF.

Once zero is established as the list terminating signal, the program must be instructed to look for it, and terminate the distance inputs. Either **if** or **while** could be used for this purpose. The first could be set to evaluate each entry: if it were not a zero, it would add it to the list; if it were zero, it would terminate data entry. This approach would require additional programming, since **if** does not have built-in looping capabilities. On the other hand, **while** does handle looping, but it can't keep the zero from being added to the list.

Within the loop, two **setq**'s were used. The first used **getreal** to accept the distance entry, and the second added the new distance to the beginning of the list using **cons**. The program assumes the user knows that OFFSET will not accept negative inputs for the offset distance. If the programmer had reason to doubt this assumption, the **getreal** could have been preceded by an **initget** with a bit value set to 5.[2]

It was decided to use **while** and strip the zero from the list. Since zero is the first item in the list, redefining the list as the **cdr** of itself would result in a list with all the entries *except* the zero.

The redefined list was then passed to **foreach** which, in turn, passed each distance to the **command** function. The OFFSET command was repeated once for each distance, thereby producing the required lines.

Study Program 4.2. Notice how the messages were handled. By defining the **getxxx** functions' messages separately, the program could be written more compactly and, if necessary, the messages can be more easily modified than if they were embedded in the selection statements.

A final word about the use of flags in programs. In this instance, we used a zero because the OFFSET command wouldn't accept that value. However, under other circumstances, zero would be an acceptable input. In that case, select an arbitrary number that isn't likely to be used as a command input (999 is frequently chosen for this purpose) and change the prompts accordingly.

4.1.3   Automatic Linear Dimensioning

All versions of AutoCAD through V.12 have required the user to select between horizontal, vertical, or aligned dimension options when dimensioning most lines. This program will enable the user to dimension to the ends of lines without having to specify the entity's orientation. (In situations where the dimension line is not parallel to the line's endpoints, it will still be necessary to specify a ROTATE dimension.) Because the program is more complex than the previous example, it will be written in a different manner.

---

[2]If the bit value is set to 1, **initget** will not allow the null input; if the bit is set to 4, negative input is not allowed. By setting the bit value to 5 (1 + 4), the programmer ensures that if the user responds with a negative value or by just hitting the return key there will be no input to the program, and the prompt will reappear.

PROGRAM 4.2—MULTIPLE OFFSETS (XOFF)

```
;|Repeatedly applies OFFSET command to a single line,
offsetting it specified distances.
                          Variables List
*************************************************************
os          Starting value of OSMODE system variable
msg1-4      Prompts for user input
d           First offset distance
dl          List of offset distances
obj         Entity to be offset
side        Side entity is to be offset to
*************************************************************
|;
(defun C:XOFF (/d dl obj side msg1 msg2 msg3 msg4)
    (setq os (getvar "OSMODE")); old value of OSNAP
    (setvar "OSMODE" 512);sets OSNAP to Nearest
    (setq msg1 "\nEnter first offset distance:  "
          msg2 "\nPick object to offset:  "
          msg3 "\nIndicate side to offset:  "
          msg4 "\nEnter offset distance or 0 to end:  "
            d (getreal msg1);first offset distance
           dl (list d);start list of distances
          obj (getpoint msg2);entity to offset
         side (getpoint msg3);side to offset
    );close of setq
    (setvar "OSMODE" os);resets OSNAP
    (while (/= d 0);as long as d isn't zero
         (setq d (getreal msg4);get next distance
               dl (cons d dl);and add it to front of list
          )
    );closes while - zero is first atom in list
        (setq dl (cdr dl));strips zero from list
        (foreach d  dl ;sets each item in list dl to d
           (command "OFFSET" d obj side "");|uses current
                                             value of d as
                                             offset distance |;
        );closes foreach at the end of the list
);closes defun
```

Short programs can be written from beginning to end and debugged in their entirety. Longer programs are best broken into individual modules that can be written and checked independently of each other. The modular approach has several advantages:

- Breaking a long program into short, useable chunks allows the programmer to concentrate on a single aspect of a complex problem at a time.

- Each section of the program can be debugged with relative ease, and once it is properly functioning, it can pass on "clean" arguments to the other sections.

- Modules can be copied and used in other programs, saving the time and effort of reinventing them.

The additional work involved in passing data back and forth between the modules is usually more than compensated for by the advantages of this approach.

Here is one approach frequently used in breaking a long program into modules:

Environment
(saving and resetting system variables)

Data Acquisition
(getting user input)

Data Manipulation
(defining new points, changing data type, etc.)

Accessing the Drawing
(doing the actual work in the drawing editor)

Environmental Restoration
(returning the system variables to their initial values)

Error Handling
(specifying what to do in case of error or unexpected program termination)

This arrangement is not cast in stone—in fact, a good case could be made for breaking the program into even smaller chunks. Some AutoLISP workers feel that if any module runs longer than a page, it should be subdivided into two or more submodules. Although every programmer does not subscribe to this concept, it does make troubleshooting a lot easier. For the present, however, let's use the six-module model.

This text will not deal with error handling within a program, so skip that module and break the program up into five subprograms. The best place to start is with the drawing accession module. That's where you'll actually specify the commands the program is supposed to apply. To use these commands, you'll probably have to specify points on the drawing. The location of these points will either be directly specified by the user or derived by the data manipulation module.

By the time you complete the data acquisition module, you'll have determined what data the user must input, and how it must be modified for the drawing accession module, so the data manipulation module will be easy to set up. SNAP and ORTHO may have to be turned off, so you have the freedom to move your cross hairs. Unless the drawing is very crowded, you may want to specify Nearest, or some other OSNAP, to make it easier to pick entities. Consider using ZOOM for a closer look. Except for ZOOM you'll have to save the current values of each of these settings and substitute the values you need.[3] These chores are handled in the environment section.

The environmental restoration module is the easiest to program. You've already determined what variables you have to deal with, so programming their restoration is simply a matter of using **setvar** to restore the variables' old values. Restoring the initial view is only slightly more difficult, even if you have gone through several views in the course of the program. One approach is to use the VIEW command and Save the initial view, then, at the end of the program, use VIEW to Restore the saved view.

The intent of the restoration module is to leave the drawing in the same state as it was when the program was initiated, except for the changes the program was designed to implement. Remember, programs that exit cleanly are more attractive to use. The more the program is used, the more time, money, or effort it will save, and the easier it will be to justify the program.

The Accession Module

To determine how to handle linear dimensioning with AutoLISP, it is first necessary to examine how it is handled by the user in AutoCAD.

The operator goes into the dimension mode and enters HORIZONTAL, VERTICAL, or ALIGNED, as appropriate. A prompt asking for the start of the first extension line or a return for an entity pick comes up. Assuming that the latter method is chosen, a line is selected, the dimension line location is specified, and the default dimension is accepted with a return. Two commands, two picks, and two returns are required for each dimension.

Data Acquistion and Manipulation

The AutoLISP procedure will first request the user to enter the distance between the line being dimensioned and the dimension line. Then the user will be prompted to select a point near (but not on) the line, on the side where the dimension line will be located. The program will then invoke the DIM1 command, select the entity, determine whether a HORIZONTAL, VERTICAL, or ALIGNED command is needed, accept the default, and place the dimension at the selected distance from the entity. Figure 4.3 shows how the XDIM command can be used for dimensioning. Program 4.3 shows the actual dimensioning program.

Data

The key to the way the program works is the selection of the point "near (but not on)" the line to be dimensioned. Call the first point P1. If P1 were a physical location on the screen and you placed your cross hairs there with OSNAP, Nearest enabled, any entity in

---

[3]If you need to restore the initial appearance of the drawing, and if no more than ten ZOOMs were used inside the program, the initial view may be restored by invoking ZOOM Previous the appropriate number of times.

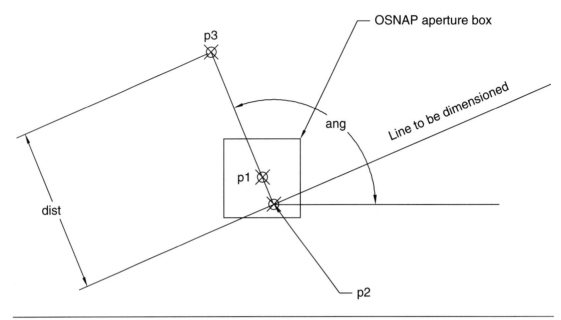

FIGURE 4.3   Dimensioning with XDIM.

the OSNAP box would be selected. In fact, a line from P1 to the selection point on the entity would form a right angle. Call the selection point P2. AutoLISP's **osnap** function simply replicates the normal selection process. Using

```
(setq p2 (osnap p1 "Nea"))
```

you can get the value of P2, a point on the line you're dimensioning.

The angle between P2 and P1 may be found without having to draw a physical line between the two points. The **angle** function will give you the angle in radians. Since the direction P2–P1 is at right angles to the line to be dimensioned, if **angle** returns 0 or π radians, the line itself will be vertical. If it returns $\pi/2$ or $3*\pi/2$ radians, the line will be horizontal. If **angle** returns anything else, the line will be oblique and will need an ALIGNED dimension. This analysis, which is done in the data manipulation module, is summed up by a variable called *TYPE*, which will have a value of *horizontal*, *vertical*, or *aligned*.

With P2 located and the angle between P2 and P1 known, P3 (which will lie on the dimension line and thus establish the distance from the object line) can be specified. Point P3 can be located by using **polar** with a start point of P2, an angle of P2–P1, and the previously entered distance as the arguments.

Accessing the Drawing

All this work will be done in the data acquisition and manipulation modules. As far as the accession module is concerned, all that is necessary is to take the data and feed it into the appropriate commands.

```
(command "DIM1" type "" p2 p3 "")
```

PROGRAM 4.3—SEMI-AUTOMATIC DIMENSIONING (XDIM)

```
;|  This program will supply a linear dimension for a line
without the user having to specify if the dimension is to be
Horizontal, Vertical, or Aligned.  It uses a single user pick
and does not permit the user to override the default value.
                        Variables List
******************************************************************
snp            Current value of SNAPMODE
os             Current value of OSMODE
ap             Current value of APERTURE
msg1-msg3      User prompts
dist           Offset distance for dimension line
p1             User pick point
p2             Point on line - derived from p1
p3             Pick point for dimension line location
ang            Angle of selected line
type           Type of linear dimension
a              Argument for dtr function
******************************************************************
end of comments
|;
      (defun C:XDIM (/snp os ap msg1 msg2 dist p1 p2 p3 type)
;
;This is the environment module
;
   (setq snp (getvar "SNAPMODE");gets current variables
          os (getvar "OSMODE")
          ap (getvar "APERTURE")
   )
   (setvar "SNAPMODE"  0);resets selected variables
   (setvar "OSMODE"    0)
   (setvar "APERTURE" 15)
;
;The data acquisition section
;
   (setq msg1 "\nEnter line-dimension line distance: "
         msg2 "\nPick a point near, but not on line:  "
         dist (getreal msg1)
           p1 (getpoint msg2)
           p2 (osnap p1 "NEA")
          ang (angle p2 p1)

;|
Data manipulation - using existing data to define a
 new points and obtain values for variables.
|;
           p3 (polar p2 ang dist)
   );close setq
   (cond
       (    ;start of first condition test
           (or
              (equal ang 0.0  0.00001);is angle close to
```

Continued on next page

PROGRAM 4.3—Continued

```
            (equal ang (dtr 180.0) 0.00001);horizontal?
        )                                    ;then
        (setq type "VER");dimension is vertical
      );                        end of first test
      (
        (or
          (equal ang (dtr 90.0) 0.00001);angle
          (equal ang (dtr 270.0) 0.00001);vertical?
        )
          (setq type "HOR");dimension horizontal
      )
      (  ;start of last test, if program reaches here
        T   (setq type "ALI");must be aligned
      );close test
    );close cond
;|The first return ("") in the next line calls up select line
option, the other return accepts the dimension value.  DIM1
exits dimension subprogram after each dimension|;
;
;Access section - uses command function to get to AutoCAD
;
    (command "DIM1" type "" p2 p3 "")
;
;Environmental restoration section
;
    (setvar "SNAPMODE"  snp)
    (setvar "OSMODE"    os)
    (setvar "APERTURE"  ap)
);closes defun
;
;|Since DTR must be available for XDIM to work, put it on the
same file as XDIM|;
(defun DTR (a)
    (setq a (* a (/ pi 180.0)))
);|When DTR is called by XDIM, the current value for ang in
the latter will be substituted for a in the former program.
When DTR is complete, the value will be returned to XDIM as
ang.|;
```

would draw a horizontal, vertical, or aligned dimension line, as specified by *TYPE,*
between points P2 and P3 with the default dimension as the value. It looks simple, but as
you can see, it embodies a lot of work.

Data Acquisition and Manipulation

The only external data needed is the distance between the object and dimension lines and
the coordinates of point P1. This being the case, it makes sense to combine the acquisition and manipulation sections.

The data manipulation module must take the data obtained by the acquisition module and locate points P2 and P3. Getting P2 is easier if the aperture box (the square centered on the cross hairs when OSNAP is active) is increased in size so that OSNAP is sure of capturing the line from point P1. Once P2 is found, angle P2–P1 and the distance are used to locate P3. The coding is straightforward:

```
(setq msg "\nSelect point near, but not on line: "
     msg2 "\nEnter dimension line offset distance: "
       p1 (getpoint msg)
       p2 (osnap p1 "near")
      ang (angle p2 p1)
     dist (getdist msg2)
       p3 (polar p2 ang dist)
)
```

The two *MSG* variables are provided with the actual user prompts. If you were writing the program from scratch, you could have entered "P1" and "Dist" instead. AutoLISP doesn't care what's in the prompts; they are for the users' benefit. Don't worry about the prompt until the program is functioning.

Since the direction P2–P1 is at a right angle to the line, use angle P2–P1 to determine the dimension line's orientation. Remember, if P2–P1 is horizontal, a vertical dimension is called for, and vice versa. If you only had to worry about two choices, **if** would be the obvious choice of function. You could check the angle; if it wasn't vertical program for a vertical dimension; otherwise, program for a horizontal dimension. Even with three choices you could use two **if**s by setting *TYPE* to "ALI", evaluating the angles, and resetting *TYPE* to "HOR" or "VER" if one of the **if** functions returned T. This approach could work with any number of choices, at the cost of increased program length. But **cond** offers a more direct approach if three or more different tests have to be run. **Cond** allows us to use multiple **Test** expressions covering mutually exclusive alternatives. Each expression is associated with a **Then** statement, which is returned by the first **Test** that evaluates as T. Since the linear dimension is limited to one of three possibilities—horizontal, vertical, or aligned—and a line can only be consistent with one of these possibilities, **cond** offers the ideal test mechanism.

The coding for determining which type of dimension line to use embodies two refinements to simplify coding and to handle the problem of lines that are almost—but not quite—horizontal or vertical. The **dtr** function (which changes degrees to radians) will allow you to use degrees rather than radians in the **Test** expressions. The **equal** function, with its fuzz factor, will enable you to treat lines that aren't exactly horizontal or vertical as if they are, in fact, horizontal or vertical. (The fuzz factor can be changed to reflect the necessary precision.)

If desired, the test angles could be given in radians (at the cost of some programming complexity) and **equal** could be replaced by = without changing the essential working of this portion of the program.

```
(cond
   ( (or (equal ang (dtr 0.0) 0.00001)
         (equal ang (dtr 180.0) 0.00001)
```

```
        );end or
        (setq type "VER"); line is vertical
    );end first test
    ( (or (equal ang (dtr 90.0) 0.00001)
          (equal ang (dtr 270.0) 0.00001)
      );end or
      (setq type "HOR"); line is horizontal
    );end second test
    (T (setq type "ALI"))
;If the line reaches the third test, it must be oblique
;by default
          );end cond
```

Notice that the last condition will always be true, so if the function doesn't return "HOR" or "VER", it *must* return "ALI". It is good practice to include such a fail-safe for **cond**, so that an exit from the **cond** function is ensured.

The Environmental Modules

The only critical environment condition for this program is having OSNAP set to None when the pick for P1 is made. If OSNAP is active, the pick point might end up on the line instead of next to it. Since SNAP might be on, and the user might have reduced the size of the OSNAP aperture box, it is a good idea to turn SNAP off and increase the box size.

Coding for these modules is simple. At the start of the program, the old values for SNAPMODE, OSMODE, and APERTURE are picked up by **getvars**. Use **setvar** statements to assign the three system variables new values (0, 0, and 15) to set SNAP off, OSNAP to None, and increase the size of the OSNAP aperture box to 15.

The last statements in the program will be another set of **setvars** to return the system variables to their original states.

Notice how the use of the **dtr** function to switch from degrees to radians makes that portion of the program easier to follow. If **dtr** were not available, 90, 180, and 270 degrees would have to be expressed as $\pi/2$, π, and $3*\pi/2$ radians and the test conditions would be more complex.

EXERCISES

These exercises involve writing the code for the data acquisition or drawing access sections for a number of AutoLISP solutions for AutoCAD applications. First determine how you would do the job in AutoCAD, then develop the AutoLISP code. As you write and test the code, you may discover shortcuts. If the results with shortcuts are comparable, feel free to use them. There is no reason AutoLISP programs have to replicate AutoCAD procedures.

1. Draw a one-unit box with its lower-left-hand corner at a user-selected point.

2. Change the last item drawn to a specified layer.

3. The XOFF program uses a 0 value (which is later stripped) as a flag to terminate the data acquisition section. Write coding such that 0 is used to terminate the acquisition section but is not added to the list.

4. A steel plate has a number of 0.755 and 0.805 radii holes drilled so that it can be bolted to a pre-existing fixture. Hexagonal bolts will be used for the 0.755 holes, while octagonal bolts will be used for the 0.805 holes. Write coding to allow the user to select a circle and have a circumscribed hexagon or octagon drawn around it without any further user input.

5. Modify the coding for Exercise 4 so that if the circle is not within 0.002 of either a 0.755 or 0.805 hole, a 1.00 circle will be drawn around it to indicate that something is wrong.

6. One useful technique in orthographic drafting is to first draw a rectangle representing the envelope of a front view. Using the front rectangle as a guide, additional rectangles are drawn in line with the front view to represent the envelopes of the top and right side views. Write coding so that the user can key in the length, height, and width of an object's envelope, and have the computer draw the appropriate rectangles in line with each other, separated by a two-unit space. The lower-left corner of the front rectangle should be at point 1,0.5.

CHAPTER 5

Writing and Debugging Programs

OBJECTIVES

After reading this chapter, you will be able to:

* Organize your strategy before coding your program.
* Encode a simple AutoLISP program using a standard word processing program, test it on an appropriate drawing, and debug it if necessary.

5.1   WRITING

Writing LISP programs is relatively easy—getting them to run correctly is the difficult part. This section will cover the procedures for writing a program, attempting to run it, correcting any mistakes so that the program runs, and ensuring that the program does what it is supposed to do. As you read this chapter, consider one of the programs covered in the previous chapter or, better yet, select a problem that you think can be solved by LISP, and apply what you learn to your own program.

When writing a LISP program to accomplish some AutoCAD task, the first step is to determine what AutoCAD commands are necessary to reach the objective. With the possible exception of the basic draw commands, most AutoCAD objectives can be reached using more than one set of commands. A line can be removed by the ERASE command or by using CHPROP to move it to a frozen layer. A screen picture can be changed by using a ZOOM or by recalling a previously defined view. An object could be drawn, inserted as a block, or inserted as a shape. Any command has advantages and disadvantages. Usually there will be a trade-off between preliminary work by the programmer and drawing effort by the user. The extent of this trade-off will be determined by the programmer's interest in the problem, the frequency with which the program will be used, and value placed on the drafter's (as opposed to the programmer's) time.

Let's assume that the best program is the one that requires the least user input. This approach gives you a measuring stick to compare programs or to evaluate a program in terms of normal user procedure.[1]

Using this approach, each possible AutoCAD strategy can be evaluated and the most effective one selected. When considering possible programming strategies, try to come up with alternatives to your usual AutoCAD practice. It is not necessary to check out all possible approaches on the AutoCAD screen, only the final candidates. These should be checked out, both to ensure that they work and, to verify that the necessary inputs and command sequences function.

Once the applicable AutoCAD approaches are decided upon, the programmer can work backward, determining the internal and external inputs required and the necessary environment for the program to function most effectively. Now it is time to start the actual writing task.

AutoLISP programs must be written in ASCII text. Unlike the usual word processing programs' output, ASCII text lacks codes for tab stops, differing type fonts and sizes, indentations, or any of the enhancements that make word processor output so attractive to use and to read. By foregoing these enhancement codes (which differ between individual publishers' word processing programs), ASCII gains a certain universality which enables it to be read by almost all word processing programs and computer operating systems.

Some word processing programs, such as the *EDLIN* and *EDIT* programs that come with various versions of the DOS operating systems, can only produce ASCII text. Most conventional word processing programs, which normally do *not* produce ASCII output, can be converted to ASCII writers by selecting the appropriate options. Normally then, it is not necessary to confine oneself to the DOS word processing programs to produce ASCII text; almost any commercial word processing package will do the job. There are also some commercial programs available, such as *M. S. Visual*, that offer enhancements that are a great help in debugging programs (such as keeping track of parentheses). There are even AutoLISP programs available for debugging other AutoLISP programs. In a sense, though, these enhancements are counter productive for the beginning programmer, since they eliminate the incentive for writing clean code the first time. Table 5.1 summarizes the most popular word processing programs that can be used to produce ASCII text.

---

[1]At this point, it should be noted that not all AutoLISP programs use AutoCAD commands, or even user input. You will run into some of these when investigating AutoLISP's use of the AutoCAD database. Nevertheless, the number of user inputs can be used to evaluate an AutoLISP program.

TABLE 5.1 Word
Processing Programs

Program	Notes
EDLIN (DOS)	Writes ASCII directly
EDIT (DOS)	Writes ASCII directly
WordPerfect	Use "Text in/out," restore using CR/LF to HRt option
Wordstar	Use nondocument mode
Microsoft Word	Save as "Unformatted"
DisplayWrite	ASCII copy to file
Microsoft Word for Windows	Use "Text Only" file format
Write for Windows	Use "Text Only" file format

With this in mind, starting programmers can use any word processing program that they feel comfortable with. The only requirement is to recall and save text in the ASCII format. As a quick check, bring up your favorite word processing program, run off a paragraph or so without using word wrap, tab stops, or any special formatting commands, then save it as an ASCII file. From the operating system prompt enter the command "TYPE" followed by your file name, file extension, and a return. If the text comes out looking more or less the way you wrote it, you can work in ASCII. On the other hand, if your screen is filled with cryptic symbols and strange formatting, you'd better check your word processing manual to see how to get ASCII text. You should also check on the procedure to retrieve ASCII files—many word processing programs will convert ASCII text to their own format if the normal retrieval procedure is used.

EDLIN, the DOS operating system word processing package, has been described as "the worst word processor ever devised by the mind of man." Nevertheless, it has two virtues that make it very useful in AutoLISP programming: it comes with DOS operating systems through Version 5.x, and, in most AutoCAD installations, it can be brought up and operated from inside the AutoCAD drawing editor. This combination makes it very effective for making minor corrections in AutoLISP programs without having to exit and re-enter AutoCAD. On the other hand, *writing* a program in EDLIN is not a job for those weak of heart. The DOS EDIT program, which replaced EDLIN in DOS 6.x, may also be entered from inside the drawing editor in any system with more than the minimum amount of available disc space, so it shares EDLIN's main virtue. But unlike EDLIN, which works on a line-by-line basis, EDIT is a full-screen editor and is easier to work with.

People differ in how they go about writing a program. Some start at the top line and work through to the last line of the program. Others start in the middle and work toward the top and bottom alternately. Some lucky souls can keep track of the variable names and inputs in their heads, others don't start writing the program until they've written a multipage outline of each step. What follows is one system. It is not necessarily the most efficient way to write a program; neither is it the worst. If you feel comfortable with some other arrangement, it is probably best to stick to it. On the other hand, if this is your first venture into programming, feel free to use the system introduced here and modify it to suit yourself.

Start with a sheet of paper listing the names of the major variables you intend to use. If the required command sequences or their options are complex, list them too. Otherwise, you can rely on your general knowledge of AutoCAD and how the program is supposed to work.

When coding a new program, try to keep things as simple as possible. Only global variables are declared. This leaves the values of all local variables accessible outside the program, a useful tool if debugging is necessary. Only minimal prompts are used and, in some instances, OSNAPs and environmental system variables are set outside the program. In this manner, you can verify the basic operation of the program before adding enhancements.

The first thing to do, when actually writing the code, is to set up the **defun** function and its parentheses. Remember, in AutoLISP the entire program must be enclosed in parentheses. However, you can easily get so involved in writing the coding for the rest of the program that you forget this essential point. So before you get carried away by the frenzy of coding, you start at the top line with:

```
(defun C:NAME ()
)
```

Then move the cursor beyond the first right parenthesis, hit the return key, and start the *real* coding.

Since the accession section is the most critical part of the program, it is the logical starting point. If **command** functions are involved, try to arrange them so that they can be stacked, thus saving memory space. If, however, the command sequence has to be broken to reset a system variable, the computer is slower processing a **command** function than a **setvar**, so set AutoCAD variables directly rather than by using a **command** function (e.g., (setvar "OSMODE" 0), rather than (command "SNAP" "off")), then re-invoke **command**. Before leaving this section, review each of the command sequences to be sure that all AutoCAD commands and options are enclosed in quotes, and that each command is terminated before data for the next is supplied. (Commands that are not self terminating, such as **layer** and **line**, should be supplied with two sets of double quotes ("") that act the same way the return key does to return to the command line.)

Once the accession section is completed, move up to the data acquisition section. At this stage, full prompts are not necessary for the **getxxx** functions, since you should already know what input has to be supplied at each step, so you can use the following approach:

```
(setq msg1 "\nPt1"
      msg2 "\nWindow"
      ......
```

```
        pt1 (getpoint msg1)
          a (getcorner p msg2)
          . . . .
)
```

The "\n" escape character places each prompt on a separate line, while the message reminds you where you are in the sequence.

If data manipulation is required, it is done immediately following the data acquisition section. Be sure the inputs to this section agree with the terms defined in the data acquisition module, and the outputs agree with those expected by the **command** sequences.

Environmental variables are recorded and, if necessary, set at the top of the program. Their initial values are restored just before the final parentheses.

In each section, you should try to use indentations to keep track of the active commands and to group similar functions. Only **defun** and its parentheses begin at the left margin. If possible, indent **setq** and **command** functions one level and arithmetic or logical functions such as *,+, or /= two levels. If logical control functions are used, try to put **Test** expressions on one line. The **Then** and **Else** statements are grouped, and if possible, uniformly indented.

While this type of formatting may take a little time (very little if it is done as the coding is written), the effort pays off when troubleshooting nonfunctional programs.

At this point the coding itself is complete. Review your work from top to bottom, looking for and correcting missing or misplaced parentheses, misnamed variables, and logic flaws in the (usually vain) hope that you can catch them all. The code is now ready for testing.

5.2   DEBUGGING

AutoLISP programs failures fall into three broad classes:

- Programs may prove impossible to load onto a drawing, thus making them impossible to use.

- Programs may load successfully, but crash when called from the command line.

- Programs can be loaded and run with apparent success, but closer examination shows that they didn't accomplish the tasks they were supposed to.

The first two types of failure are attributable to flaws in the application of AutoLISP, and are the primary concern of this section. The fault for the third type of failure lies with the logic of the program. Either because of incorrect inputs or poor use of AutoCAD in **command** functions, the program cannot function as designed. The cure for this situation lies in a rigorous, step-by-step examination of what the program is supposed to do from the AutoCAD rather than the AutoLISP standpoint.

Programs are loaded onto drawings by typing (load "NAME") at the AutoCAD command line. "NAME," in this instance, must be a valid name for an ASCII file with a .LSP file extension, and must include, if necessary, path information. (The .LSP file extension is *not* included in NAME.) If the computer cannot find the specified file, it obviously cannot load it. Therefore, the first thing to do in this situation is to double-check the file name, file extension, and path. (Remember there is no requirement that the name of the .LSP file must agree with the name of the function. In fact, as we will see later, many AutoLISP files contain several functions.) Then use the DOS "TYPE" command to make sure the file is in ASCII format. If it is not in ASCII format, check your word processor to see if it converts your non-ASCII text to ASCII (most can). As a last resort, retype your program, this time making sure that it is saved as an ASCII file.

The usual reason that properly named and formatted AutoLISP files fail to load is that either the number or arrangement of parentheses (or quotation marks) in the file is incorrect. At this point, even the most casual reader must realize that AutoLISP programs include a great number of parentheses. (In fact, there are many people around who believe that LISP stands for *L*ost *I*n *S*tupid *P*arentheses). The numbers and location of these parentheses are critical to the functioning of AutoLISP programs. To add to the problem, AutoLISP is programmed not to evaluate anything between quotation marks. For example, if a program includes the improperly coded line

```
(setq a (getstring "Enter the name of the drawing ))
```

everything to the right of "Enter . . . will be assumed to be a prompt until the program encounters the next quotation marks. Because the closing quotation marks are omitted, the line actually contains two opening and *no* closing parentheses as far as AutoLISP is concerned.

If a parentheses error is encountered while attempting to load an AutoLISP program, an error message is issued. This message may be in one of three forms. A greater than symbol (>) followed by a number indicates the number of missing right parentheses, the number of quotation marks, or both. An "error: malformed list" message is issued when, because of missing parentheses or quotation marks, one or more functions are run together. Finally, if there are *extra* right parentheses, a message to that effect is issued. In all three cases, the solution is straightforward but tedious.

The first step in the correction process is to obtain a paper copy of the program in question. This may be obtained either by printing it as an ASCII file, or by copying the file, renaming it, and converting the renamed file to a non-ASCII file using a word processing program. The paper copy must then be examined for unpaired parentheses and/or quotation marks. You may find the following approach useful, but if it doesn't appeal to you, feel free to use any method you choose.

1. Examine all the prompts and **command** function lists for missing quotation marks and correct if necessary.
2. Check for the opening and closing parentheses of the **defun** statement and pencil in a bracket connecting them. Be sure that a pair of parentheses immediately follows **defun**. They must be present, even if empty.

3. Go through each of the multilined functions (stacked **setq**s, **if**s, **cond**s, **while**s, **com-mand**s, etc.) and bracket their opening and closing parentheses. Here's where indentations pay off.

4. Examine the remaining single line functions and keep a count of the parentheses. Increase the count by one for every left-hand parenthesis, decrease the count by one for every right-hand parenthesis. At the end of each line, the count should be zero. If it is not, check to see that a parenthesis that should have been bracketed in Step 3 was included. If this isn't the case, then parse the line checking each function on it to be sure that it is logically complete.

Once the missing quotation marks and parentheses are entered, it might be a good idea to run another hard copy and repeat the counting process.

The most difficult type of debugging occurs when the AutoLISP program loads, but crashes when an attempt is made to run it. When this happens, the function that was current when the program crashed appears on the prompt line, followed by the functions that called the current function. Unfortunately, the current function is not necessarily the cause of the crash. "Indirect" bad input as a cause of crashing presents a good argument for breaking programs up into short modules. If a given module crashes, it could be run on a stand-alone basis, with good data supplied directly. If the crash is not repeated, the fault lies with the data modules. On the other hand, if the module still crashes with good data, the problem must lie within the module itself. Knowing that the problem lies within a single module makes troubleshooting a lot easier.

The usual cause for a function's failure is insufficient or bad data. If this is the case with the current function, the real cause of the crash lies with the data supplied to it, not the function itself.

If the crash occurred during an AutoCAD command, examine the input to the pertinent **command** functions at the command line. If necessary, you can bring it up by switching to the text screen. Are the commands getting the correct values for the variables used? Are the values coming in the proper sequence? Sometimes the fault lies with the previous command. If, for example, the last command was a LAYER command and the program didn't return to the command line (by including a closing "" in the **command** string), AutoCAD will be expecting a valid response to the LAYER command, instead of one for whatever the current command is.

If the **command** functions check out, the fault may lie with the values assigned to the AutoLISP arguments. If you followed the advice given earlier and did not declare local arguments, you'll be able to check their values by entering each argument, preceded by the exclamation point, at the AutoCAD command line. As each value is returned, check it. If it is "nil" you know something is wrong; if it is non-nil, you'll have to go deeper.

If the declaration statement looks satisfactory, but the argument still comes up "nil," check the spelling in the declaration statement and anywhere else the argument is used within the program. Computers are very literal devices. They see no relationahip between p1, pone, and p-one, so a misspelled or misnamed argument will come up "nil" (but remember, PONE and pone are equivalent). If you see any such mismatches, correct them.

Even if the argument does have a value, it may still be at fault. Is the argument of the proper type? Strings will be returned between quotes, and real numbers will have at least one trailing decimal. What about the values? Have you tried to divide by zero or committed some other type of mathematical error? Backtrack each argument to its first appearance in the program and verify that everything is correct.

If you can show that all the arguments are correct, the next step is to investigate the functions used in the program. Some functions, notably **command** and **setq**, may be stacked; others, such as **setvar,** cannot. Unfortunately, there isn't any listing that tells you whether or not a function can be stacked. If you get a message about "too many arguments," you may want to go back and unstack everything except **command**s and **setq**s. While you're at it, check that each function and argument is set off by a space or a parenthesis.

If you're using any new or unfamiliar functions, be sure that you are using them properly by bringing up AutoCAD and checking them, one at a time, from the command line. Even if the function in question is a user-defined one that has worked in the past, you may be working from a corrupt copy, or you might have forgotten some critical detail about the function.

Finally, go back and check all your previous debugging efforts—it may save you a lot of work in the long run. If all else fails, there is always the "brute force approach." Here is one version of this method:

1. Get a hard copy of the program, then open a new file. Type in the **defun** function with the opening and closing parentheses and a pair of empty parentheses for the arguments.

2. Go to a line between the arguments' parentheses and the closing parenthesis, and type in all the statements in the environment section of your program.

3. Switch to AutoCAD and load the program on an empty drawing.

4. Invoke the program by entering its name at the command prompt, either by itself (for C: programs) or between a pair of parentheses. In the latter case, enter the values for any required arguments for the environment section.

5. If the program runs, check to see that the required setting changes were made. If they were made, skip to step 7.

6. If the program does not work, you'll know that there is at least one program error in the environment section. Knowing approximately where the error is, you can find it, correct it, and check it by reloading the program on the drawing and running it.

7. Correct your copy of the complete program so that it exactly agrees with the tested module and try running it. If the only error was in the environment section, the complete program should run. If not, enter the data acquisition section.

8. Repeat the procedure for each of the other modules in the program, putting the new module after the previous ones and in front of **defun**'s closing parenthesis. Once the last module has been checked out, you'll have a functioning version of the program. You can discard the first complete copy of the program and substitute the coding you've just typed up.

The brute force approach should not be your first choice for fixing a nonfunctioning program. But if you can't find the problem using more conventional methods, try it.

Even if your program runs, you still have a few chores to do. Now that the program is running correctly, you no longer need access to the local arguments for debugging. Declare them by entering their names in the argument list following the **defun** statement. (Be sure that your argument list agrees with the arguments used in the rest of the program.)

Check the prompt messages: now is the time to beef them up so that you, or others, will be able to use the program in the future. It might be a good idea to have an outsider use the program with you as a silent observer. This is an excellent way to identify ambiguous prompts.

When the arguments are properly listed and the prompts changed, load and run the program again to make sure that you haven't introduced any new errors.

The final step in writing a program is documentation. Proper documentation of a program is very useful if the program is going to be upgraded, used by others, or altered to fit changing circumstances.

The starting point for documenting a program should be the working papers you used in writing the program. If you needed variable lists, verbal or pictorial flow charts, and notes on unusual programming techniques to write the program, those who follow in your footsteps need them to understand your approach to the problem.

Comments can be added to the .LSP file using semicolons (;) for single-line entries and the ;| . . . |; combination for multiline explanations. Some users object to including comments with a .LSP program on the grounds that they needlessly enlarge the file, thus taking up more memory. Programs have been developed to strip semicolons from .LSP files, thus shortening complex program files. However, complex programs are ones most likely to need extensive documentation, so purging comments does not seem to be a particularly good approach. An alternative method is to convert a copy of the "XXX.LSP" file to a text file, add the documentation, and run off a hard copy for archival use. This documents the program, but archival files may be lost or unavailable to a user having trouble with a given program. The combined approach is probably best: put the necessary documentation on a .LSP file *and* produce a text file of the program with more extensive documentation. If comments are added to the .LSP file, the program should be checked out a final time, just in case a semicolon was misplaced or omitted.

EXERCISES

The exercises for this section are essentially expanded versions of the ones in Chapter 4. In each case, make up a complete program including appropriate environment sections and complete prompts. Use your work from Chapter 4 as a starting point.

1. Draw a one-unit box with the lower-left corner at a user-selected point. To make sure that the box is completely on a 12×9 screen, modify your program so that the pick point cannot have an X coordinate greater than 10.5 or a Y coordinate greater than 7.5. Make the grid and snap settings one unit, and return these setting to their initial values at the end of the program.

2. Set up a program to change selected entities to a selected layer. Assume that the specified layer doesn't exist the first time you set up the program. Include coding to make the layer and set a flag so that the next time the program is used, it will not attempt to make an already existing layer.

3. Create a program to place AutoCAD POINT entities on the screen at specified locations (build up a list of point lists) and connect the points with LINE entities. Since the points are to be visible, change the default value that governs the point type.

4. Use a procedure similar to the one used in Exercise 3 to build up a list of the centers and diameters of a number of circles with diameters of either 0.755 or 0.855. The smaller circles are to be surrounded by a circumscribed hexagon, and the larger ones by a circumscribed octagon. Set the program up so that the user can specify the center location and diameter each hole, then have AutoLISP set a flag that will indicate if the hole is to be circumscribed by an octagon or a hexagon. *Hint:* Specify each hole with a four-atom list in which the first two atoms are in a sublist representing the X and Y coordinates, the third atom the diameter, and the fourth, the flag.

5. Assume that you are starting a drawing and have three properly sized rectangles representing the front, top, and right side views of an object. These rectangles have been drawn following the specifications in Chapter 4, so the length, width, height, and locations of the rectangles is known. A hole, represented by a circle in the front view, is drawn. Write a program that will draw the lines representing the hole in the top and side views. The lines are to be drawn within the rectangles, not through the spaces separating them.

CHAPTER 6

Using AutoLISP for Communications

OBJECTIVES

After reading this chapter, you will be able to:

- Use AutoLISP commands to print messages on a screen and data to an ASCII file.
- Use AutoLISP commands to extract data from a file in a form such that it can be assigned to a variable for use in an AutoLISP program.

Although its primary concern is with graphics, AutoLISP must be capable of communicating both with the current user and, occasionally, with other computers. In some circumstances, the messages must be preserved as hard copies, but they may also be saved as electronic ASCII files. Fortunately for the user, the same basic techniques and commands are used regardless of the destination of the message. These commands are summarized in Table 6.1.

6.1 ACCESSING ASCII FILES WITH AUTOLISP

All file input/output requires the specification of a file with a "file descriptor." The file descriptor is *not* the same thing as the file name. The file name is a readable descriptive title for the file, with or without a three-letter file extension. However,

TABLE 6.1 Commands for Printing to Screens and Files

Function	Notes
(ascii str)	Returns the ASCII code for the first character in string *str*.
(chr int)	Returns the character whose ASCII code matches the integer *int*.
(close f-desc)	Closes file identified by file descriptor *f-desc*.*
(graphscr)	Switches from the text to the graphics screen in single screen system. No effect on two screen set-ups.
(open "filename" "mode")	Opens a file for access by I/O functions and returns a file descriptor (not the file name). File name (including extension) must be enclosed by quotes. Mode must also be quoted, may take values of "w" (write), "r" (read), or "a" (append).
(prin1 [exp[f-desc]])	Prints expression verbatim on screen, or, if *f-desc* is present and represents a file open for writing, prints to file.
(princ [exp[f-desc]])	Similar to prin1, except control characters included in (chr) function are expanded (e.g., (chr 10) gets printed as \n). If control character itself is included, it controls the output (e.g., \n produces a new line, \t tabs the text to the right).
(print [exp[f-desc]])	Similar to prin1, except a newline character is inserted before *exp*, and a space is added after *exp*.
(prompt msg)	Prints *msg* verbatim; *msg* must be a string.
(read-char [f-desc])	Returns ASCII code of character in open file specified by *f-desc* or from keyboard buffer. Repeated read-char calls will return subsequent characters.
(read-line [f-desc])	Reads string from keyboard or open file, similar to read-char. Returns nil if end-of-file character is encountered.
(terpri)	Prints a new line on the screen.
(textpage)	Turns on text screen in single screen systems. Clears existing text from text screen.
(textscr)	Similar to textpage, except doesn't clear existing text. Equivalent to AutoCAD's flip screen key.
(write-char num [f-desc])	Writes character with ASCII code *num* on screen or to specified file if it is open for writing
(write-line str [f-desc])	Writes string to file, omitting quotation marks. File must be open for writing.

*The file descriptor is not the same as the file name. The descriptor is an arbitrary code assigned when a file is opened. See the discussion below.

78

when AutoLISP opens a file for the first time, it assigns the file an identifying number[1] just the way it does any other entity. This number serves to identify the file for the duration of the drawing session or until the file is closed. To refer to the file, one must use the number, since AutoLISP doesn't recognize the file name. Keeping track of the identifying number is easy: simply assign it to an AutoLISP variable. For example:

```
(setq output (open "test.txt" "r"))
```

will assign the number for the file TEST.TXT to the variable, *OUTPUT*, which then becomes the equivalent of the file descriptor number for that file. Once the file is opened for reading it could be accessed with a series of commands such as

```
(read-line output)
```

or

```
(setq text (read-line output))
```

Every repetition of either of those commands will either bring one line of text to the screen or assign it to the variable, *TEXT*. If access to the full file is needed, it can be obtained by retrieving the file on a suitable word processor using its assigned name, in this case, TEST.TXT.

Whenever the file is reopened, the process repeats itself. The new identifying number is assigned to the variable (in this case, *OUTPUT*), and lines or single characters are either read into the file or from it with the appropriate commands using the same variable to supply the value of the new number.

A few words of warning are appropriate here for readers who may have forgotten, or are unaware of the basics of file handling:

1. Every time a file is opened for writing, any data on it is lost, so to add data to an existing file, use the "a" (Append) mode.

2. Some programs and text editors write text files with an end-of-file (EOF) marker (CTRL Z, ASCII code 26) at the end of the text. When DOS sees this symbol, it returns an end-of-file status, even if additional data is on the file. This means that if you are using a file produced by one of these programs you must purge the EOF symbol before letting AutoLISP open the file in the "a" mode.

3. Every file that is opened must be closed. Failure to do so may corrupt the file and plays hob with the hard drive. In theory, any open files will be closed when exiting from AutoCAD, but it is much better to play it save and use the **close** command within the same AutoLISP program that opened the file.

4. The "a," "r," and "w" modes, (as well as all the letters in AutoLISP's format control codes, discussed below) must be in lowercase.

---

[1]The identifying number is in a hexadecimal (base 16) format, so, in addition to the usual 0–9 figures, it may also contain the letters A, B, C, D, E, and F. The number associated with an AutoCAD entry may be used to access information about it. See Chapter 8.

TABLE 6.2   Format Control Codes

Symbol	ASCII Code	Meaning
\\	010	Prints \ character
\"	034	Prints " character, useful for putting quotation marks *inside* strings
\e	027	Prints escape character for ANSI[*] sequences
\n	010	Newline character, moves next line of text down and to the left margin
\r	013	Return character, moves to left margin
\t	009	Tab character
\nnn		Prints character whose *octal*[†] code is nnn

[*] Used with ANSI.SYS, a DOS system level device driver.
[†] Octal codes use characters from 0 to 7. To convert from decimal to octal, divide the decimal by 8, write down the remainder, then divide the rest of the quotient by 8, and write the remainder to the left of the first remainder. Repeat until the quotient is less than 8, and then write the quotient as the left-most digit of the octal number (e.g., $231/8 = 28$ with a remainder of 7, $28/8 = 3$ with a remainder of 4, so $231_{10} = 347_8$).

When in AutoCAD, special characters may be invoked by preceding them with a pair of percentage symbols (%%). These characters give AutoCAD users the capability of using symbols that aren't normally available from the keyboard such as the degree symbol (%%d), the diameter symbol (%%c), and over- or underlining within the text (%%o and %%u). If the user has defined special entities called SHAPES and included their definitions in the current font file, they too may be accessed using %%nnn (where nnn is the ASCII code for that symbol). The %% codes cannot be used in AutoLISP text, but formatting can be specified and special shapes called up by using AutoLISP's format control codes, summarized in Table 6.2.

6.2   CONTROLLING OUTPUT TO SCREEN OR FILES

The formatting codes are AutoLISP representations of commands that are issued in real time from the keyboard. For example, when a user hits Enter or the return key, the computer receives the commands to return to the current left margin and move down to the next line. In a DOS system, this is represented by ASCII character 10. (Other operating systems may use a different character, or may issue two separate codes, one to move to the left, the other to move down.) If a format code (for example, \t) is embedded in an AutoLISP string, it is interpreted as a formatting instruction and acted on by the **prompt, princ,** and **write-line** commands, but **print** and **prin1** will simply print the code verbatim. Formatting codes may also be entered using the **chr** function and the appropriate ASCII code. However, if **chr** and the code are embedded between the quotation marks of a string, they will be ignored. They cannot be added before or after the quotes, since the functions we are discussing expect a string or a single item as an argument. This problem is handled by a function, **strcat,** which is discussed in the next section. Simply put, **strcat** concatenates (combines) strings and (more importantly in the present context) **chr** functions into a single string. **Prompt, princ,** and **write-line** will act on codes entered with **chr,** while **print** and **prin1** will insert the appropriate formatting codes but not act on them.

Both the **chr** function and \nnn-type format codes can be used to invoke shapes and special characters. Remember, however, that while the **chr** function uses a decimal value for the ASCII code number, the \nnn-type format code must be converted to an octal value.

You're probably wondering why the developers of AutoLISP found it necessary to devise so many ways of providing output to a screen or file. They did so to provide the user with an arsenal of commands to handle output in a variety of ways. The easiest way to understand this is to examine how each of these commands works on the same string (Table 6.3). But before getting to the specifics, there are a few general rules to keep in mind.

TABLE 6.3 File and Screen Outputs from Print and Write
Commands (setq a "This is \n a test")

Command*	Screen Output	File Output
print a	(new line) "This is \n a test"	(new line) "This is \n a test"
(prin1 a)	"This is \n a test"	"This is \n a test"
(princ a)	This is a test	This is a test
(prompt a)	This is a test	Not applicable
(write-line a)	This is a test	This is a test

*File descriptor omitted.

Notes: The **write-char** function accepts only ASCII codes, so it is omitted from this table. Also omitted is **terpri,** which can only be used to return a blank line to the screen. In all cases, if the listed function is the *last* one in a program, it will print "This is \n a test" on the screen.

1. Most screen output can be handled with **prompt** and the prompts for the **getxxx** functions.

2. **Prompt** can only handle strings sent to the screen, and **write-line** can only output strings to either the screen or a file. On the other hand, **print**, **princ**, and **prin1** can handle any type of expression and can output to files as well as to the screen. **Write-char** takes an ASCII character code as its argument.

3. If they are the last function in a user-defined function with screen output, **prompt**, **print**, or **prin1** will print either nil or their argument at the command line. Sometimes this confuses the user, so it is best to terminate your programs with **terpri** or **princ** (without any argument) to ensure a clean exit.

4. **Print** adds a new line in front of the data, and inserts a space after it. This improves the appearance of data sent to and then read back from a file.

Usually when AutoLISP writes data to a file, it is with the intention of retrieving the file into an AutoLISP program. But there are times when all that is desired is a printed copy of the data. Consider, for example, a part with a large number of holes to be drilled in it. The intention is to have the drilling done by a either a manual drill press or a tape-driven numerically-controlled press which is incapable of direct translation of the drawing database into positioning data. (Most *C*omputer *N*umerically *C*ontrolled machine tool software programs are capable of translating AutoCAD drawings into appropriate machine coordinates and directly controlling the machine in question.)

The aim of the program is to create an ASCII file that, when printed out, will give the press operator the diameter and center of each hole. This information is obtained by setting OSNAP to Quadrant and instructing the user to pick the top and bottom of each circle (Figure 6.1). The identical X coordinates of the two picks and the average of the Y coordinates give the center of each hole, and the difference between the Y coordinates yields the hole's diameter.[2]

After turning off SNAP and setting OSNAP to quadrant, the program initializes a counter then opens up a file for input.

The program first writes a header to the file. The header embodies multiple \n characters to print the hole number, diameter, X coordinate, and Y coordinate under each other, thus replicating the way the actual quantities will be written to the file. This enables the user to decipher the numbers on the printout.

This example uses a vertical file format; that is, each item of data is set on a separate line. Later, we will see how to format the data into space- or comma-delimited horizontal files, which look better and occupy less space on the output page. However, if

---

[2] In a later chapter we will discuss a method for finding a circle's radius and center with only one pick. The two-pick method is used here because it can be applied to regular polygons. See Exercise four, at the end of this chapter.

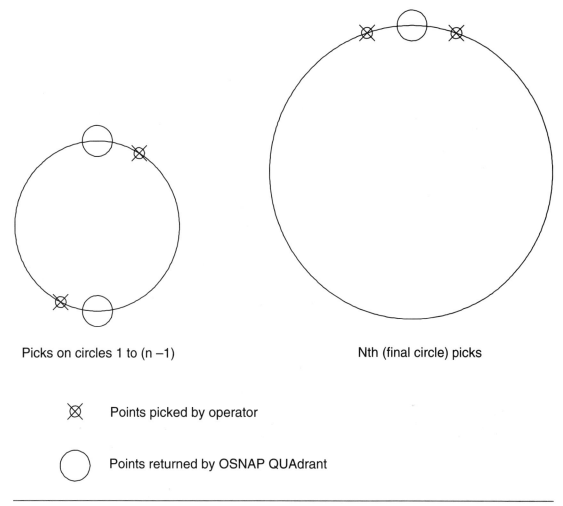

Picks on circles 1 to (n −1)   Nth (final circle) picks

⊠   Points picked by operator

◯   Points returned by OSNAP QUAdrant

FIGURE 6.1   Pick points for CIRCDATA.

the data in question is to be read and used in an AutoLISP program, it might be better to stick to the vertical format, where each data item can be recovered by a single **read-line** function. In the standard horizontal format, each character in the line would have to be checked to see if it is a comma or a space—a slow process.

Selecting the points, calculating the diameters, and locating the centers of the circles is done within a loop. The current data is converted to strings and written to the file during each pass through the loop with **write-line** functions. A **princ** function with a new line format character provides an extra blank line to separate the data from different holes.

The loop is closed by picking the same point twice. Since the program is already beyond the **Test** expression when the double pick is made, the data from the double pick is written to the file. However, since the reported diameter for these picks is equal to zero, the user can ignore the last set of data.

Once the program exits the loop, the file is closed and the system variables SNAPMODE and OSMODE are restored to their initial states. The required hard copy is produced outside of the program, either by copying the file "CIRCLES.TXT" to the printer port or by calling the program up in the ASCII mode on a word processor then sending it to the printer.

Setting up the **Test** expression for the **while** loop requires a bit of thought. At the start of the program, both P1 and P2 have a value of nil, since they haven't been bound to anything. Since both have the same value, an **=** or **equal** function will return true, thus terminating the program. Using an **or** function and including a test for a zero value for the counter (*NUM*) will enable the program to go through its first cycle without terminating the loop. After the first cycle, both P1 and P2 will retain their last values and thus be different, so even though the variable *NUM* isn't equal to zero, the **Test** expression will not return true until the same point is picked twice in a row. The **equal** function was used instead of **=** since successive picks (even with OSNAP active) may not return exactly the same coordinates. The actual program is shown with annotation as Program 6.1.

Upon close analysis, a flaw may be noted in CIRCDATA. Since the **while** loop includes a command to print data to the file, all of the data, including that developed by the double-pick used to terminate the program, will end up on CIRCLES.TXT. This means that the file will contain one extra entry, a circle with a diameter of 0.000. Normally, an entry such as this will not cause any problems, since any reasonable individual will recognize that it is impossible to drill a hole with a 0.000 diameter.

There are two schools of thought on how to deal with such a problem. The first school feels that the best thing to do is to insert the few lines of code that would solve the problem. The second school feels that, since there will always be nit-picking, why not leave a known, easy-to-dispose-of nit?

Either way, the question of whether to accept a working program with known flaws or to spend the time to eliminate them is far from being a trivial one. On one hand, perfection is always preferable to close-to-but-not-quite-perfect. On the other hand, it may be better to submit a program with documented flaws than to keep everyone waiting while you run down a trivial problem. There is no easy answer to this problem, but there is room for compromise. In the case of CIRCDATA, this could mean modifying the program to print something like "DISREGARD THE LAST LINE" as the last entry on CIRCLES.TXT, and letting the program be used while you try to eliminate the flaw.

Material that is read into a file is useless unless it can be retrieved. Although there is an array of functions available for writing to a file, only two functions are available for reading: **read-line** and **read-char**. **Read-line** can be used to read a line of text or data back to an AutoLISP program as a string. **Read-char** returns the ASCII code of each successive character to the screen. For example, if the only item in a file called

PROGRAM 6.1—SENDING DATA TO A FILE (CIRCDATA)

```
;|This program determines the location and diameter of any
number of circles and sends it to a specified file.

                         Variables List
=================================================================
num           Counter
snp           Initial value of SNAPMODE system variable
oos           Initial value of OSMODE system variable
msg1-3        Prompts
out           Identifier for file
pt1, pt2      Pick points at quadrants of circles
dx            X coordinate of circle's center
dia           Diameter of circle
dy            Y coordinate of circle's center
sum           String representation of num
=================================================================
|;
(defun C:CIRCDATA ()
   (setq  num    0
          snp    (getvar "SNAPMODE")
          oos    (getvar "OSMODE")
         msg1   "\nSelect point near top of circle   "
         msg2   "\nSelect point near bottom   "
         msg3   "Double click on top to exit"
          out   (open "CIRCLES.TXT" "w");tag for file
   )
;Print up heading for file
     (princ "NUMBER\nDIAMETER\nX-COORD\nY-COORD" out)
     (princ "\n" out)
     (setvar "OSMODE" 16);Osnap set to quadrant
  (while
        (or
;Points are not the same
          (not (equal pt1 pt2 0.00001))
          (= num 0) ;counter set to 0
        );loop continues until both return nil
      (prompt msg3);shows up for each cycle
      (setq pt1 (getpoint msg1);top of circle
           pt2 (getpoint msg2);bottom of circle
            dx  (rtos (car pt1));X coordinate of center

; Diameter by subtracting lower from upper Y coordinate
           dia  (rtos (- (cadr pt1) (cadr pt2)))
;        Center by using average of Y coordinates
            dy  (rtos (/ (+ (cadr pt1) (cadr pt2)) 2))
           num  (+ num 1);increments counter
           snum (itoa num);converts to string
        ) ;closes setq
```

Continued on next page

PROGRAM 6.1—(Continued)

```
      (write-line snum out ) ; writes snum to file
      (write-line dx out);writes x-coord to file
      (write-line dy out);writes y-coord to file
      (write-line dia out);writes diameter to file
      (princ "/n" out);blank line
  );closes while
  (close out);shuts file - a must!
  (setvar "SNAPMODE" snp);reset snap
  (setvar "OSMODE" oos);reset osnap
  (princ);closes program with clean command line
);ends function
```

"TEST.TXT" is the word CAT, and the following programming sequence is applied to the file:

```
(setq try (open "TEST.TXT" "r"))
        (repeat 4
     (read-char try)
        )
        (close try)
```

the computer will return 67, 65, 84, and nil. These are the ASCII codes for C, A, and T, **read-char**'s response to the end-of-file marker. That last item is the important one. We can use **read-char** to check each character on a line of a file before asking **read-line** to pull the line back to AutoLISP. When **read-char** returns nil, it signifies that the end of the file has been reached. We can then get out of the loop that was causing **read-line** to repeat and get on with the rest of the program.

6.3   EXTRACTING DATA FROM FILES

Many times, users aren't interested in a line-by-line playback of a file—they simply want to look at the *entire* file all at once. If this is the case, the most efficient procedure is to get back to DOS and use "TYPE," followed by the file name and path to look at the file as an entity. If the file is too long to fit on a screen, most systems will show a screen at a time if the file name is followed by the following sequence "| more". In that case, the file can be viewed a screen at a time, by hitting any key to move to the next screen. Finally, as is the case with any ASCII file, it can be printed out on a properly configured printer. You can use the DOS copy command to send the

TABLE 6.4 String Functions

Function	Notes
(strcase str f1)	If f1 is present, converts all characters in *str* to upper case. If f1 is absent, converts to lowercase.
(strcat str1 str2 . . .)	Returns a string consisting of concatenation of *str1, str2* . . .
(strlen str)	Returns length of *str* (w/o quotes).
(subst new old list)	Searches list for old substring, returns list with new in place of old.
(substr str strt [len])	Returns *len* long substring of *str* starting at *strt*. If *len* absent returns substring from *strt* to end of *str*.

file to the printer port, or you can load the file on a word processor (using the ASCII procedure if you're going to use AutoLISP on the file in the future) and go through the print commands.

As previously mentioned, AutoLISP offers only two ways to get data *from* files: **read-line** and **read-char**. Because **read-char** can read only one character at a time, the burden of pulling data from files falls on the **read-line** function. Since **read-line** can only return strings, AutoLISP has provided a number of string functions to deal with extracting and manipulating data from files. These are summarized in Table 6.4.

Once the data string is retrieved, it may still have to be converted into a real or fixed value, depending on the use it is put to. We have already met the **atof** and **atoi** functions, which convert strings into fixed or integer values respectively. The **read** function is more flexible. **Read** returns the first list or atom from a string verbatim, so if that atom is a numerical value it will be returned either as a real or integer value, reflecting the value that was read into the string. If the string in question contains blanks, only the first "word" is returned, unless the string contains a pair of the \" format control characters (which will, in a sense, produce a string within a string). However, **read** cannot "force" data into a specified format, so if a real number is entered without the decimal, **read** will return it as an integer.

Strcat is another highly versatile function. It returns a string which is a concatenation of a number of strings or variables representing strings. For instance, in a previous example, we were forced to supply data in a vertical (one item per line) format. If we wanted to use a horizontal format to print out a real and an integer value from a vertical file described by the descriptor, *F1*, one approach might be:

```
(setq valuea (read-line f1)
      valueb (read-line f1)
```

```
          a " "; blank spaces
          b (atof valuea); forces a real value
          c (atoi valueb ); forces an integer value
          d (strcat "THE VALUES ARE:" a b " AND" a c)
          )
    (print c)
```

This would print the following line:

```
  "THE VALUES ARE: 23.456 AND 232"
```

on the screen, assuming, of course, that 23.456 and 232 were the values for *VALUEA* and *VALUEB*. If the **print** function had a file descriptor, the same approach could be used to produce a horizontally formatted file which, when printed out, would be in a readable form accessible to an operator. However, since 23.456 and 232 are now embedded in a string, they would not be accessible as data items for another computer program without some additional manipulations.

   If the output is to be read by another program, each data item must be extractable by the program in the appropriate format. That is, the user program must be capable of extracting each field on the record and reading all the records in the file. In view of this, the user program requirements must be known before the program to write the file is written, otherwise a lot of time will be wasted trying to put square pegs into round holes.

   One widely used approach is to require that each item in a record be separated from its neighbors by a *delineator*, a specified character used to tell the receiving program that it has reached the end of an item. Spaces (ASCII code 0) and commas (ASCII 44) are the most widely used delineators. Files with delineators can be read by AutoLISP, but it is a slow process.

   Suppose you want to extract a series of numbers stored in a comma-delineated format on a single line of a file. A file with the descriptor *TRIAL* is opened for reading and **read-line** produces the following which has been assigned to the variable *A*:

```
"2,3.45,8.234,91,0.002"
```

This line can be broken into seven data items by reading each individual character until a comma is reached, then repeating the procedure until the end of the line is reached. The ROUT program diagrammed in Figure 6.2 will do so, producing an AutoLISP list that can be passed on for use by AutoCAD commands.

   In the first section of the program, a dummy list (*LST*) and a dummy string (*STR*) are set up. The string consists of a pair of double quotes and the list contains a pair of parentheses. As each character is read from the file, it is checked to see if it is a comma, and, if not, it is added to the string with the **strcat** function. If the character is a comma, it signifies that the dummy string now contains one complete data entry, so the string, represented by the variable *OUT*, is added to the existing list by means of

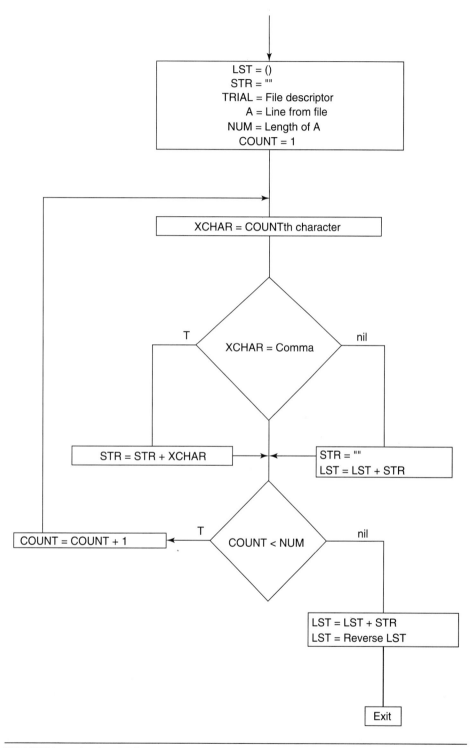

FIGURE 6.2   Logic of ROUT.

the **cons** function.[3] At the same time, the string represented by the variable *STR* is redefined as a pair of double quotes. The first section also opens the file, reads a line of data, sets it to *A*, and determines the number of characters in the line (*NUM*).

The next section uses the **repeat** function to go through the string *NUM* times. Each character is extracted by **substr**, which sets the variable *XCHAR* to a one-character substring beginning at the current value of *NUM*.

XCHAR is then checked to ensure that it isn't a comma and it is added to the end of *STR*. If *XCHAR* is a comma, *STR* is added to *LST*, and *STR* is redefined as an empty string. Since the output list is created by adding each substring to the front of the existing list, the resulting list will be reversed relative to the line extracted from the file. The list is reordered with the **reverse** function, and the dummy character is extracted by redefining the list as the **cdr** of itself. The final list consists of a correctly ordered series of sublists, each consisting of a single data entry in the form of a string. These string lists may be converted to simple strings by using the **caar** function to extract them. The resulting strings may be converted to either real or integer values with the **read** function. Study Program 6.2 in its entirety to see how data is extracted from a file using the ROUT function.

An alternate approach goes back to the early days of general-purpose computers, when programs were punched onto "IBM" or, more properly, "Hollerith" cards. These cards were set up so that each punch mark could be identified by its horizontal "row" and vertical "column." Each character of the information entered onto the card was represented by one or more punch marks placed in specified columns. For example, an individual's name might be entered as punch marks in columns 8 through 28, his or her sex could be represented by a single punch mark in column 29, and age could be represented by punch marks in columns 32 (units), 31, and, optimistically, 30. A similar approach applied to an AutoLISP readable file might use the **substr** function to pick up the values in positions 8, 29, and 30 so as to report the name, sex and age from each line of the file. Assuming that data was set up as a string called *STR*, as shown below:

```
"1234    Smith, John Q III      M059"
```

with "S" being the 8th character in the string, "M" the 29th, and "0" the 30th, the following coding will extract the data in a computer useable form:

```
(setq name (substr str 8 20)
      sex (substr str 29 1)
      age (atoi (substr str 30)) ;convert to integer
)
```

---

[3]*OUT* must be converted to a list before being acted on by **cons**, otherwise it would produce a dotted pair that would be unuseable for data extraction.

PROGRAM 6.2—EXTRACTION OF DATA FROM A FILE (ROUT)

```
;| This function parses an ASCII file on a line-by-line basis, and
produces a list containing the individual atoms making up each line.

                             Variables List
=====================================================================
lst         A list to contain the individual atoms
str         String holding individual characters comprising the
            data atom
trial       File identifier
a           Variable containing one line from file
num         Number of characters in line a
=====================================================================
|;
(defun C:ROUT  ()
  (setq   lst   (list);sets up dummy list
          str  "" ; sets up dummy string
        trial   (open "TEST.TXT" "r")
            a   (read-line trial) ;reads line from file
          num   (strlen a) ;length of line
  )
  (repeat num
    (setq xchar (substr a num 1)) ;isolates Numth character
      (if
          (/= xchar (chr 44)) ;|if xchar is not a comma
                               it is added to the dummy string|;
            (setq out (strcat str xchar))
            (progn
;|if xchar is a comma, the string is added to the dummy list and
then reset as an empty string|;
              (setq lst (cons (list out) lst)
                    str   ""
              )
           );closes progn
        );closes if
   );closes repeat
(setq lst (cons (list out) lst));adds last (NUMth) value to lst
;|
 The list now consists of sublists, each containing one item of
data as a string.  The data items are in reverse order.
|;
    (setq lst (reverse lst));list now in correct order
);end of function
```

Since no length was specified for the **substr** function used to extract *AGE*, the characters from position 30 to the end of the string were returned. Because the first item (1234) was not required, there was no need to extract it or to have the computer needlessly parse positions 1 through 7.

EXERCISES

1. You have written a very complex program that requires a great many instructions to the operator. Demonstrate how you would get the program to print out six or seven lines of instructions so the operator could see all the lines at once and read them—several times, if necessary—before going on with the program.

2. Using AutoCAD, draw a circle, a line, and an arc on the screen and place some text next to each entity. On paper, take note of the commands, options, and points used, then erase the entities. Write the information to a file as a comma-delineated string, then write a program to read the file and use the input to redraw the entities by assigning them to variables which, in turn, are used by **command**. (Since DTEXT requires keyboard input, it will not work from AutoLISP or scripts, so use TEXT for the labels.)

3. Repeat Exercise 2, this time using a word processor in the ASCII mode to set up the file in Hollerith format.

4. The CIRCDATA program used two picks to locate a circle's center and determine its radius. Using a similar approach, write a program to find the center and circumscribed radius of a regular hexagon.

CHAPTER 7

Practical Programming II

OBJECTIVES

After reading this chapter, you will be able to:

- Break down a complex program into understandable parts for typing or debugging a code.
- Use subfunctions to receive, redefine, and pass on arguments.
- Use template strings to control string input.
- Develop a UDF that will call up two or more UDFs that will, in turn, make a simple drawing and change its color, layer, or linetype.

7.1   BREAKING DOWN COMPLEX PROGRAMS

Beginning programs tend to be simple, short, and easy to debug. The next level introduces a complexity that may be difficult to cope with. Besides the problems associated with figuring out the coding for more complex programs, there are problems associated with typing and debugging the code. What follows is a technique for minimizing the trauma associated with more complex programs.

As you have seen, breaking a program into sections makes it easier to design, write, and check out the program. The core of the program, including the AutoLISP commands needed to accomplish the given task, can be written, fed the necessary date (by using

setqs to set variables' values), and checked out. Since the coding involved in this case is minimal (compared with the coding for the entire program), this approach makes it easier to locate errors. Once the accession coding is known to be free from errors, the data acquisition section can be written and checked. Then the entire program can be written and verified in this piecemeal manner.

This same piecemeal approach may be applied to a complex program, but with a twist: Instead of writing each subprogram as a separate section, write it as a separate function. If the function in question does not have a leading C:, it can include arguments as well as local symbols. Function arguments can be passed on to other functions and can be used to carry out the work of a complex program. To see how this works, go back to the program you used to draw a box. This program took two points as input, used them to calculate the four corners of a box, then drew a line connecting the points and forming the box. Suppose we have defined the following function:

```
(defun XXBOX (a b)
      (setq p1 a
            p2 (list (car b) (cadr a))
            p3 b
            p4 (list (car a) (cadr b))
      )
      (command "LINE" p1 p2 p3 p4 "C")
)
```

Then the following program would draw a box:

```
(defun C:XXBOX ()
      (setq p1 (getpoint "Pick lower left corner: ")
            p2 (getpoint "Pick upper right corner: ")
      )
      (xxbox p1 p2)
)
```

Xxbox is defined with AutoLISP's **defun** function. The definition starts off with a name for the function to be defined. From a practical standpoint, this name should be short, should imply what the function will do, and should not duplicate the name of any existing AutoLISP function or AutoCAD command. The name is always followed by a pair of parentheses that may contain a listing of the variables used by and within the function. If a variable is included in this list, it is said to be a declared variable. It is not necessary to declare any or all of the variables used in a function. There are two types of declared variables. Both types are listed in the same set of parentheses. If both are present, they are separated by a slash (/) with spaces preceding and following it. Table 7.1 shows the differences between the two types of declared variables as well as undeclared variables. The coding for the function follows the obligatory parentheses, and, except for a closing comment, the last character in the definition is the closing parenthesis for **defun.**

Returning to the fragment that called up **xxbox**, notice that names of the variables representing the two points in **xxbox** are not the same as the names used in the definition

TABLE 7.1   Use of Variables in Functions

Variable	Designation in Function Definition	Characteristics
Argument, External variable, Global variable*	In front of the slash, e.g., (A1 A2 / L1 L2)†	Value must be supplied when the function is invoked. The value may change inside the function but will revert to the initial value upon exiting the function.
Local symbol, Local variable*	To the right of the slash, e.g., (/ L1 L2)	Value is defined inside the function; it is not available after exiting the function.
Undeclared	Not included in function definition	Value may be redefined within the function, latest value is accessible after exiting the function.

*Argument and Local symbol are the terms used in the AutoLISP release 12: AutoLISP reference. Undeclared variables are not discussed.

of **xxbox**. It wouldn't have made any difference if the names were the same. **Xxbox** simply takes the first value passed to it (P1 in this case) and substitutes it for the first argument in its definition A. In a similar fashion, P2's value is substituted for B's as **xxbox** calculates the location of the four points. To put it another way, functions such as **xxbox** disregard the actual names of the variables passed to them. They simply use the order in which the variables are received.

Thus, by using subfunctions to receive, redefine, and pass on arguments, even the most complex programs may be broken down into easily digestible chunks. Using this approach, the main function, the one preceded by C:, is used only to call up the necessary functions, as in the example below:

```
(defun C:MAIN (/ a b c d e f g)
  (setq a 1 b 2 c 3 d 4 e 5 f 6 g 7)
    (subfun1 a b c);accepts and redefines a, b, c
    (subfun2 a c e f);uses new values for a, c
    (subfun3 f g)
);end defun
```

Remember, functions such as **C:main** may only have local symbols (i.e. to the right of the slash) associated with them. Functions such as **subfun1** can have both arguments and local symbols assigned to them. In fact, AutoLISP will permit you to list a variable both as an argument (in front of the slash), and as a symbol (e.g., **funname** (a b / a c x y). . .), a useful trick if you want to conserve memory space. However, while you're writing a UDF or a program, do *not* declare any symbols or arguments. This will allow you to get the value of all the variables involved even after exiting the program—a useful capability when trying to track down an error!

Once the initial plunge into using subfunctions is made, several other possibilities open up. If you've been following the suggested approach of breaking complex functions into environment, acquisition, manipulation, access, and restoration sections, you've probably become aware of a certain amount of repetition in the individual sections of different programs. Many of the sections differ only in small details. If subfunctions are used, it is possible to develop a group of universal functions that can be used for *every* program. These subfunctions are most useful for the environment, acquisition, and restoration sections, since these require the least modification when used in different programs.

7.2   DATA ACQUISITION FUNCTIONS

Although the **getxxx** functions can be used by themselves to acquire the necessary data for a program, this approach leaves them open to accepting improper input, such as negative numbers for counts. Up to now, this hasn't been too important, since it can be assumed that the programmer is aware of what constitutes good or bad inputs. But this situation changes as the programs become more complex.

Complex programs generally accomplish more than simple ones and are more likely to be used by people other than the programmer. Once the program leaves its creator's hands, the problem of improper entries is likely to raise its ugly head. This problem can be solved by adding filters to the input functions.

For example, the coding:

```
(setq flag 1)
  (while (= flag 1)
   (setq count (getint "Number of times"))
   (if (>= count 1)
     (setq flag 0)
   )
)
```

will not accept a nil input or any input less than one. If presented with anything but a positive integer equal to or greater than one, it will repeat the prompt until it gets an acceptable value.

If we embody the coding in a function, such as:

```
(defun xxint (message)
   (setq flag 1)
```

```
(while (= flag 1)
  (setq count (getint message))
      (if
        (>= count 1)
        (setq flag 0)
      )
  )
)
```

then a positive, nonzero response could be guaranteed by the following coding.

```
(setq msg "\nEnter a number = or greater than 1")
(xxint msg)
```

As long as the input requirements are relatively simple, this approach is effective. It does, however, require that a new **Test** expression be written for each filtered input. In addition, it is a clumsy approach for handling strings, since all acceptable responses must be written out (e.g., if a "yes" response is required, the test string must include "Y" "yes" and "YES" as well as all possible combinations of the upper- and lowercase letters "Y," "E," and "S").[1]

The combination of **initget** and a **getxxx** function will filter out unacceptable responses with much less effort on the programmer's part. **Initget** uses a decimal representation of a binary number to designate unacceptable numerical inputs. The meanings of each of the code values are given in Table 7.2.

The codes may be added for composite effects. For example if null values, negative values, and 0 are unacceptable inputs, a bit code of 7 (1 + 2 + 4) would be used. If zero were acceptable, a code of 5 would be used. The **initget** function must be above the user input function it is to control, and must be reset for each subsequent function. Using **initget**, the **xxint** function could be replaced with:

```
(setq msg "\Enter number of cycles ")
(initget 7)
(setq count (getint msg))
```

A user who enters a value less than 1 will receive the message "Value must be positive and nonzero." Although the **getint** function is repeated when an unacceptable response is keyed in, it is *not* necessary to reset **initget**, because **getint** is never satisfied, and therefore never uses up the **initget** setting.

The 128 code is something of a wild card. When used alone, it will accept anything as an input. For example, it will accept Roman numbers as input to a **getint** function. It is probably better to avoid using bit code 128 unless you're sure that your users will submit

---

[1]The **strcase** function could be used to change the response to either all uppercase or all lowercase letters, but this would merely cut the number of strings to be incuded in **initget** by a factor of 2. All the variants of "YES" would still have to be included to ensure an acceptable input.

TABLE 7.2   Numerical Control Values for Initget*

Bit Value	Action
1	Rejects null input
2	Rejects input of zero
4	Rejects negative input
8	Allows entry of points outside of limits
32	Rubber bands cursor on graphics screen
64	Disallows Z coordinate inputs to getdist
128	Allows arbitrary input, honors other keywords and control bit (except 1)

*Values may be added to combine effects.

only numerical input as responses to numerical **getxxx** functions. If that's the case, the 128 code may be combined with any other bit code except 1 to filter inputs.

Initget will not work with **getstring**, but if **getstring** is replaced by **getkword**, string input may be controlled. The **initget** controlling a **getkword** input may also include a one-bit code to prevent the user from just hitting the return key and having the resulting null string accepted as input.

The string option of **initget** uses a template string to assess string input. If the input matches the template, it is accepted; otherwise it is rejected. There are three possible forms for the template string. In the simplest, the acceptable strings are written as a lowercase string consisting of the acceptable input(s) separated by spaces, for example:

```
(initget "length width height")
```

A **getkword** function following such an **initget** statement would only accept the words "length," "width," or "height" in upper- or lowercase letters as input. If acceptable input wasn't supplied, the user would be prompted for input again.

The second—and most useful—possible form of the template string uses uppercase letters to specify the minimum acceptable abbreviations. If the input matches the uppercase letters, the uppercase letters and any or all of the following letters, or the complete word, it will be accepted. If, for example, the **initget** function string was written as:

```
"LENgth wiDth heigHT"
```

the next **getstring** would accept "len," "leng," "lengt," "d," "dt," "dth," or "ht" as well as the complete words. Again, either upper- or lowercase letters may be used.

The third form of the template string requires acceptable words to be written out in full in uppercase letters, followed by a comma and the acceptable abbreviation (which can only be the initial letters of the word). In this form:

```
"LENGTH, LEN"
```

would accept the same responses for length as the second form, but there is no way to specify the equivalent of "wiDth" or "heigHT."

User input functions may also include default values which will function the same way as AutoCAD's defaults. The key to using this feature is the fact that AutoCAD's defaults are all strings—even the numerical values. The coding below shows one way that this can be used to force a **getxxx** function to accept a default.

```
(setq a (getreal "Default ");numerical default
      msg "\nEnter a number" ;prompt message
  )
    (if (= a nil);if no default
        (setq msg msg);use prompt message
        (setq msg (strcat msg " <" (rtos a) ">"))
;Add default and brackets to initial message
        )
        (setq b (getreal msg);prompts with current msg
        (if (= b nil)(setq b a);accepts default
      );closes if
```

Again, this coding could be converted to a function with the default and message as arguments by omitting the first **setq** statement. If a function similar to the coding above and called **xnum** was created and used with a default value of 2 and "Enter a number" as the message, the call:

```
(setq b (xnum 2 msg))
```

would issue the following prompt for *B*:

```
"Enter a number <2>"
```

while (xnum nil msg) would prompt with "Enter a number".
In both cases, the value for *B* would be available to the rest of the program.

There is, however, a problem with using **initget** and a default simultaneously. If **initget**'s bitcode disallows a null return it will be impossible to enter the default by just hitting the return key. If the default is to work as we want it to, we cannot have a 1 (the code for disallowing a null return) in the bitcode. Since any bitcode containing 1 will be an odd number, the obvious solution is not to use odd numbers for bitcodes when a default is present. But suppose the programmer isn't aware of this problem and uses an odd number. Is there a way we can have the input function correct the situation? One solution is to have the program subtract one from the bitcode. But if the bitcode were even, this would make it odd, creating a problem where none existed before. So what we need is some code that subtracts 1 only from odd numbers. But if no default is present, we may really want to disallow null inputs, so the remedial coding will have to subtract 1 only if a default is present and if the bitcode is odd. Below is one way of solving the problem. The code assumes that the default and bitcodes are represented by *DEF* and *BIT*.[2]

---

[2]*BIT* must have an integer value. Using **fix** will prevent an inadvertent real causing a crash, but for simplicity's sake, **fix** will not be used in this section.

```
(if (and (def)  ;if a definition is present
    (/= bit (* (/ (fix bit) 2) 2)))) ;and bit's odd
    ; an odd integer divided, then multiplied, by 2 will not
    ;| equal itself |;
        (setq bit (1- bit)) ;reduce bit by 1
  ) ;otherwise leave it alone
) ;close outer if
```

Program 7.1 puts the whole thing together and sets up a function that will tell the user to enter a controlled numerical value, supply a default, and keep prompting the user to supply an acceptable input. The function must be supplied with values for the bitcode (*BIT*), the default string (*DEF*), and the prompt (*MSG*).

If you wish, you may directly assign the UDF's output to a variable. This is done by replacing the last four lines of the code in Program 7.1 with:

```
(if val val def)
```

which will return the value of *VAL* if it is anything but "nil" and the value of *DEF* if the return key was entered at the prompt. If this procedure is used, **xreal** must be placed inside an assignment statement, such as:

```
(stq xlength (xreal bit def msg))
```

PROGRAM 7.1—USER-DEFINED INPUT FUNCTION (XREAL)

```
        (defun XREAL (bit def msg)
            (initget bit)
:|If a default is present, check the value of bit, and change
it if the value is odd|;
            (if  (and   (def)
                        (/= bit (* (/ bit 2) 2))
                ) ;closes and
                (setq bit (1- bit)
            ) ;closes if
;|If a default is present, the next five lines of code will put
it into the prompt message, if no default is present, a colon
and spaces will be added to the message|;
            (if def
                (setq msg (strcat
                    msg "< "(rtos def) ">:   "))
                (setq msg (strcat msg ":   "))
            ) ;closes if
             (initget bit) ;uses adjusted value
             (setq out (getreal msg))
;|If the response is a return, the value of OUT is set to the
default.  For any other response, OUT is set to the entered
value.|;
                (if
                    (= nil out)
                    (setq out def)
                ) ;closes if
) ;closes function
```

Although this may seem like a lot of coding just to use **getreal** inside a program, there are a number of good reasons to consider this approach. First, this function enables you to control user input of real numbers with only one line of code:

```
(setq output (xreal bit def msg))
```

provided, of course, that you've already assigned values to *BIT*, *DEF*, and *MSG*.

Second, **xreal** can be used as a starting point for other numerical input functions. By changing the **rtos** function used to make the default a string to **itoa**, **xreal** could be converted to **xint** to accept integers. By substituting **atos** for **rtos** you could set up a **xreal** type function to accept angular inputs.

The same approach could also be used to control string input, although it's less flexible than **getstring**. The **initget/getbword** combination can accept only single-word responses, while **getstring** can accept spaces without terminating the input as long as the flag is set to a non-nil value. Use **getkword** when the operator has only a limited number of options or when you want to force a non-nil response (set the bitcode to 1). If you do use **getstring** and have to filter the responses, it's a good idea to use **strcase** to change all the responses to either upper- or lowercase. Remember, as far as AutoLISP is concerned (= "Yes" "yes") is *not* true. Don't forget to use the double quotes on all your strings in the **Test** expressions.

A final word about input UDFs. In setting up **xreal** and all the other UDFs derived from it, use two **if** functions to check whether a default is present. The first one changes odd bitcodes to even values, and the second reconfigures the prompt to include the default. This makes the logic clearer and it makes the program easier to debug. You can also accept the default values for **rtos** just to keep things simple.

A single **if** can be used and the default and the prompt can be reconfigured within a single **setq**. This is possible because if an integer value is acted on by

```
(* (/ bit 2) 2)
```

it will return the initial value if the starting integer is an even number, and one number less than the initial value if it is odd. The coding below, a more polished version of **xreal**, eliminates the second **if**, sets the default to a two-place decimal, and puts a carriage return in front of the prompt.

```
(if def
  (setq msg
    (strcat "\n" msg " < " (rtos def 2 2) ">: ")
      bit (* (/ bit 2 ) 2)
 );setq
  (setq msg (strcat "\n" msg ": "))
);if
```

If this coding is combined with an **initget/getxxx** combination, the input will be limited to acceptable values.

7.3   THE ENVIRONMENT SECTION

Since the environment section is a series of simple **setq**, **getvar**, and **setvar** statements, it would seem that writing a function to handle each of these sections would be easy: Just supply a looping function with a list of AutoLISP variables and a list of system variables, then equate the two. Unfortunately, it doesn't quite work that way. The hard part is setting up a list of AutoLISP variables. Variables are not strings, so they can't be quoted. If they're set up as a list of alphabetic or alphabetic/numeric characters, AutoLISP will evaluate them and return a value of nil. What is needed is a method of generating variables to be matched as needed to a list of system variables inside the loop.

Let's assume you have a program that requires snap and drag to be off, the grid to be set to 2, 1, and a center OSNAP. This will first require you to get and save the current values of the system variables: SNAPMODE, DRAGMODE, GRIDUNIT, and OSMODE. Then set these variables to 0, 0, (2 1), and 4, respectively. Finally, at the end of the program, you want to restore the four system variables to their initial values.

The program to do this requires three lists: (1) a list of the variable names you wish to assign to each system variable's value; (2) a list of the system variables you are dealing with; and (3) a list of the values you wish to be in place while the program is active. The first list will be used when you extract the values of the system variables at the start of the program and reset them at the end of the program. The second list is used to extract the values, reset them to the desired values, and restore them at the program's end. Since these two lists will be used repeatedly, it's a good idea to assign them to dummy variables that can be broken down in each of the three programs leaving the initial lists intact.[3] The third list is used only once—to set the system variables during the program—so it isn't really necessary to use a dummy variable.

The specific lists needed for the program are shown below:

```
;current values of system variables in quoted list
      (setq olval '(osnp odrag ogrid oosmod))
;names of system variables in quotes
(setq sysvr '("SNAPMODE" "DRAGMODE" "GRIDUNIT" "OSMODE"))
;values to be used during program
      (setq nval '(0 0 (2 1) 4))
;dummy lists
(setq xolval olval xsysvr sysvr xnval nval)
```

---

[3]An alternative would be to declare each of the lists as a global variable so that any changes made inside the subprogram would be negated upon exiting. However, this may make debugging more difficult.

   Program 7.2 assigns the current value of each of the listed system variables to the
corresponding member in the *XOLVAL* list. You'll have to use the **car** function to get the
first value from *XOLVAL* and then strip the first value by redefining *XOLVAL* as the **cdr**
of itself. But a statement such as:

```
(setq (car xolval) . . .)
```

presents problems.

   When the **setq** function was first introduced, the point was made that the "q"
could stand for a single quotation mark which would prevent the function from evaluating the term immediately following **setq**. But in this case, the term in question is the
list (car xoval), which is meaningless in the context of **setq**. (That's because (car xoval)
is a function list, not a variable, and you can't assign a value to a function list.) What is
needed is a function that will get the value of (car xoval); in other words, a function
that will evaluate the second atom in the list. Now, if the reason **setq** doesn't work in
this situation is that "the q invokes a quote which prevents evaluation," what about getting rid of the q? If we drop the q from **setq** we end up with **set**—a function that does
evaluate the second term in the list. It is quite possible that the operational coding
evoked by **setq** has no relation to the coding for **set**, but from the user standpoint, the
two functions may be treated as if **setq** was **set** with a quote.

   The **repeat** function is probably the best looping function to use for all three of
the environment subfunctions. The only input that would be required in addition to the
lists already discussed is the number of items in any one of the lists (they're usually
all the same length). Since few programs will require resetting more than a half dozen
system variables, the number can be entered with **setq** just before the program is
called.[4]

   Entering "(xtract xolval xsvar 4)" from the command line will set each item in
XOLVAL to the value of the corresponding system variable in *XSVAR*. In this instance, since

---

PROGRAM 7.2—EXTRACTION OF SYSTEM VARIABLE VALUES (XTRACT)

```
(defun xtract (a b num)
   (repeat num
      (set (car a) (getvar (car b)))
      (setq a (cdr a) b (cdr b))
   );closes num
      )
```

---

[4]The AutoLISP function **length** will return the number of elements in a list and can be used to minimize operator input.

PROGRAM 7.3—ASSIGNMENT OF NEW VALUES TO SYSTEM VARIABLES (VARIN)

```
:|This program takes preexisting lists of system variables, values
and sets each member of the first list to the corresponding value
in the second list.|;

    (defun varin ( / x y)
         (repeat num
;Takes 1st item from each list and equates them
             (setq x (car xsvar) y (car xnval))
                (setvar x y)
           ;redefines list bringing up new item in first position
             (setq xsvar (cdr xysvar) xnval (cdr xnval))
         ); closes repeat
      );ends function
```

---

the lists themselves are global, they emerged unchanged from the program, but the items inside *XOLVAL* are assigned values.

The program for setting the variables to the new values (Program 7.3) and the program for restoring the old values are essentially the same, differing only in that the former uses lists *XSVAR* and *XNVAL* while the latter uses *XSVAR* and *XOLVAL*. Since nothing is set to a variable from a list, the coding is simple. The code sets the system variables to their desired values. It assumes that *NUM* has been assigned a value and the two lists have been redefined to their original forms.

The dummy variables *X* and *Y* are necessary because **setvar** is expecting a quoted system variable and a value to set it to, not a **car** of lists containing these quantities. *X* and *Y* could be declared local variables, since their only function is to serve as place holders.

7.4   DATA MANIPULATION

For the most part, data manipulation is a straightforward affair. The data is acquired through a **getxxx** function and manipulated with the appropriate functions. There are, however, a few UDFs that can be used at this stage to reduce the programming burden.

The **rtd** and **dtr** functions, which relate angular measurements to their radian counterparts, are one type of function that can be useful for handling previously acquired data. Another kind of function that is helpful includes stripper functions. These functions take a data list and remove each element of the list in turn. Look at the function below:

```
(defun strip ()
    (repeat num
       (setq a (car lst)
             lst (cdr lst)
       )
      )
)
```

If it is supplied a list (*LST*) containing *NUM* elements, this UDF will set each NUM element in turn to the value of *A*. If *LST* were a list consisting of a number of sublists, **strip** would assign a sublist to *A*, and the sublist could be subsequently be broken down using **car**, **caar**, **cdr**, and the like. Later in this chapter we will use a **strip**-type UDF to draw a line through each point specified in a list of point lists.

7.5   UDFs AND DRAWING ACCESS

Because this section of a program is usually unique to the program, the use of UDFs as canned programs is limited. There are a few exceptions, however. If, for example, a program requires a complex command sequence that is used more than once in the program, it might make sense to make up a simple UDF that executes the command. In most cases, AutoCAD dialogue boxes are suppressed when a command is accessed with AutoLISP so, in order to maintain consistency, use the mnemonic abbreviations that appear in uppercase letters when the command is accessed from the command line inside the **command** function. For example, if a program frequently has to move the last drawn entity to a layer called "PARK," the following function could be used:

```
(defun C:PARK ()(command "CHPROP" "L" "" "LA" "PARK" ""))
```

Remember to close the selection set with a pair of double quotes, and be sure that you use the mnemonics from the command line *not* the ones underlined in the dialogue box.

Defining a function imposes an overhead burden on AutoLISP's memory resources. Most of the time, this burden is justified by the efficiencies brought about by the UDF, but there are exceptions. For instance, if a programmer realizes the need for a UDF while writing program code, the main program must be put aside while the UDF is written. For the programmer, this could be an interruption in working out the program's logic. More importantly, for someone who is trying to *understand* the program, the need to refer to the UDF is an unwelcome break in the logical sequence. The **lambda** function is AutoLISP's attempt to enable programmers to define functions "on the fly" so as to avoid the burden of defining a UDF and to embody the mechanisms of the function at the point in the program where they are applied. **Lambda** functions are frequently used with the **apply** function and/or with **mapcar** to perform operations on the members of a list or lists of values, as outlined in Table 7.3.

TABLE 7.3   Apply, Lambda, and Mapcar Functions

Function	Notes
(apply func list)	Executes *func* on all the elements of the list
(lambda arg exp)	Subjects each element of *exp* to the operations specified by *arg*
(mapcar fun lst1 . . .)	Executes *func* on all the elements of the specified lists

Although experienced programmers use **lambda** functions along with **apply** and **mapcar** as needed, at this stage of the game, their advantages do not offset the effort required to set them up. At least with a UDF, once you have it working right, you can use it anywhere you want to. **Lambda** functions are strictly one-shot deals. Loops can be set up to replace **apply** and **mapcar** to perform repetitive operations if needed.

AutoCAD Version 12 supports the use of AutoLISP with the PRINT command, and PLOT sequences take enough time to make good candidates for automation. PLOT is an exception to the rule that AutoLISP suppresses dialogue boxes. If the system variable *CMDDIA* is set to 0, PLOT commands can only be entered on the command line or through AutoLISP. (Don't forget to reset *CMDDIA* at the end of your program!) If you're using an earlier version of AutoCAD, you can use the **command** function to call up script that will supply the printer settings, but you can't use the PLOT command. In AutoCAD V.12, PLOT is directly accessible from AutoLISP.

Another use for UDFs when accessing the drawing is in troubleshooting more complex programs. If the program's flaw lies in the command sequence, UDFs using the **command** function can be used to isolate the difficulty. The necessary data is entered with **setq**s from the command line, and checked by entering an exclamation point and each variable from the command line. Once the data is known to be correct, the appropriate UDF is written to go through each command until the incorrect coding causes a crash. At this point, knowing what the wrong coding is, entering the correct coding is relatively simple. In fact, you can use this approach in the planning stage of programming to see if a given command sequence does what you want it to.

To get a sense of how the subfunction approach can be blended with the method you've been using up to now, let's take a look at Program 7.4, which combines both approaches. This program is a graphing program intended for students who are essentially not computer literate. The program is intended to produce a graph showing experimental results and a "best fit" curve embodying the results on the screen. The graph will be viewed by the instructor who, if it is satisfactory, will use DTEXT to label the graph and the axes and PLOT to print the graph.

PROGRAM 7.4—ON-SCREEN GRAPHING (XGRAPH)

;| This program draws two dimensional graphs in the first quadrant
from user-supplied data. The graphs are scaled so that the slope
can be measured with some accuracy. The data points and axes are
shown, and a smooth curve is drawn to indicate the probable
relationship between the variables.

Upon completion, the graph may be annotated and plotted by using
AutoCAD's DTEXT and PLOT commands outside the program.

Variables List

a, b, c	1) Prompts for setting type of curve
	2) Arguments for user-defined functions
bit	Control for initget, insures positive, nonzero value
count	Counter
def	Default value for X and Y values
flag	1) Holds message on text screen until a value is entered
	2) Determines if X or Y coordinates govern scaling
kwd	Sets permissible inputs for type of curve
llim	Lower limit of drawing extents
lr	Length of X axis
msg	Prompt for type of curve or point
nlst	List of scaled data points
num, xnum	Number of points (num), number of points minus 1 (xnum)
npts	Number of data points
oll	Initial value of LIMMIN system variable
olval, xoval	List and substitute list of old system variables
opm	Initial value of PDMODE system variable
ops	Initial value of PDSIZE system variable
ost	Inital value of SPLINETYPE system variable
oul	Initial value of LIMMAX system variable
pnt1	CAR of point list (xpln)
pnt2	CADR of point list (xpln)
ptn	Data point
ratio	Scaling factor
svar, xsvar	List and substitute list of replacement system variables
type	Value of SPLINETYPE variable to control curve type
ul	Length of Y axis
ulim	Upper limit of drawing extents
val	Holder for values in user-defined functions
varin	User-defined function to set system variables
xaxis	User-defined function to draw axes and tick marks
xdist	Spacing for tick mark on X axis
xint	User-defined function to input integer values
xkword	User-defined function to control string input
xpl	Last data point
xpln	List of data points

Continued on next page

PROGRAM 7.4—(Continued)

```
xpline       User-defined function to draw PLINE
xpoint       User-defined function to place point entity on
                 each data point
xreal        User-defined function to input real number
xscale       Scaled value of maximum X value
xtract       User-defined function to save current system variables
xval         Largest X value
xxpt         Scaled value of data point
ydist        Spacing for tick mark on Y axis
yscale       Scaled value of maximum Y value
yval         Largest Y value
|;
;
(defun C:XGRAPH ( / a b bit c count def flag kwd llim lr msg nlst
num npts oll olval opm ops ost oul pnt1 pnt2 ptn ratio svar type ul
val varin xaxis xdist xint xkword xnum xolval xp1 xpline xpln
xscale xsvar xval xxpt ydist yscale yval)
;DATA INPUT SECTION
;
(textpage);Brings up clear text screen
;Maximum X and Y values
    (setq bit 7 msg "Enter largest X value  " def 10)
    (xreal bit def msg)
    (setq xval val);Largest X value
;|Since there's been no exit from XGRAPH, BIT retains its last
value  |;
    (setq def 7 msg "Enter largest Y value:  ")
    (xreal bit def msg)
    (setq yval val)
;|The next line prints three blank lines - if princ were absent,
"nil" would be printed on the third line |;
    (terpri) (terpri) (terpri) (princ)
  ;Entry of number of data points
  (setq def 10 msg "Enter number of data points: ")
  (xint bit def msg)
  (setq npts val)
  (terpri) (terpri) (terpri) (princ)
;Selection of spline type
(setq a "Curve fitting may be done with either a cubic or a"
      b "quadratic function.  Cubic gives a smoother curve"
      c "but quadratic curves stay closer to the data points"
    msg "Cubic or quadratic fit?  (C/Q)"
    def "Cubic"
    kwd "Cubic Quadratic"
)
;|Print explanatory material, then two blank lines and prompt.  The
contents of variables A, B, and C may have to be adjusted to fit
the screen width  |;
  (prompt a) (prompt b) (prompt c) (terpri) (terpri) (princ)
```

PROGRAM 7.4—(Continued)

```
(xint bit def kwd msg)
(setq type val)
(textpage); Clears screen after data for xint is entered
(setq a "ENTER OR PICK POINTS IN SEQUENCE - FOR KEYBOARD"
      b "ENTRY, ENTER X COORDINATE, A COMMA, THE Y COORDINATE"
      c "THEN THE RETURN KEY"
)
(prompt a) (prompt b) (prompt c)(terpri)(princ)
;|The text shown above must remain on the screen long enough for
the user to assimilate it.  Input to the next setq function will be
assigned to a dummy variable (which will be redefined later in the
program), as soon as the getstring is executed, graphscr will bring
up the graph screen for entry of the data points|;
;
(setq flag (getstring "Hit any key to continue"))
(graphscr)
   (setq   xnum (1- npts)
         count 1
   )
   (repeat xnum
      (initget 1)
      (setq msg (strcat
          " \nPick or key in point " (itoa count) ":    "
                 )
             ptn (getpoint msg)
             xpl (cons ptn xpl)
           count (1+ count)
       );close setq
   );close repeat
   (initget 1)
    (setq msg "\nPick or key in last point:    "
          ptn (getpoint msg)
          xpl (cons ptn xpl)
    )
;DATA MANIPULATION SECTION
;Setting scaling factor
   (setq xscale 1 yscale 1 a xval b y val)
       (if (> b a)
          (setq flag 1)
       )
       (setq ratio (/ b a))
;|Setting scale factors so that the largest values are equal to the
nearest tenth.  Precision is set by converting to a one-decimal
place string, then changing string back to a real.|;
          (if (= flag 1)
              (setq yscale (atof (rtos (/ 1 ratio) 2 1)))
              (setq xscale (atof (rtos ratio 2 1)))
          )
; Length of axes set 10% longer than largest X or Y value
          (setq   xval (* 1.1 xval xscale)
```

Continued on next page

```
                            yval (* 1.1 yval yscale)
                              ur (list 0 yval)
                              lr (list xval 0)
                            xdist (/ xval 10.0);forces real value
                            ydist (/ yval 10.0)
            )
;Scaling data
;|The X and Y coordinates of each point in XPL are multiplied by
XSCALE and YSCALE to form a new point which is added to the list
NLST.  When the end of XPL is reached, NLST is redefined as XPL|;
      (repeat npts
            (setq xxpt (list
                    (* xscale (car xpl))(* yscale (cadr xpl)
                        )
              );scales each point
                    nlst (cons xxpt nlst)
                      xpl (car xpl)
                  )
          )
      (setq xpl nlst)
;Conversion of Quadratic/Cubic to 5/6
        (if (= (strcase type) "QUADRATIC"))
;value of TYPE converted to uppercase by strcase function
            (setq type 5)
            (setq type 6)
        )
;ENVIRONMENT SECTION
(setq olval '(oul oll ops opm ost)
  nval  (list (car lr)(cadr ul)) '(0 0) 5 2 type)
  svar  '("LIMMAX""LIMMIN""PDSIZE""PDMODE" "SPLINETYPE")
    num   5;Number of system variables involved
  )
;Duplicates lists olval and svar so that they can be used twice
  (setq xolval olval xsvar svar)
;Extraction of old values
(xtract xoval xsvar num);Assigns old values to "o" variables
  (setq xsvar svar);Reconstitutes XSVAR
;Setting new values
  (xvarin xsvar nval num);Sets system variables
;
;DRAWING ACCESS
;
(command "ZOOM" "A"    ;Zooms to limits
          "ZOOM" ".9X" ;Moves axes in from side and bottom of screen
  )
;Drawing and splining pline
(xpline)
;Drawing axes and tick marks
(xaxis)
```

Continued

PROGRAM 7.4—(Continued)

```
;Putting AutoCAD point on each data point
(xpoint)
;Restoration of old system variable values
; (xvarin svar oval num);Restores old variable settings
);Ends XGRAPH function
;
;
;The following section includes the UDFs required for XGRAPH
;
;|You must supply values for all the global arguments listed in
these functions.  If they aren't needed in a specific instance,
supply null values, such as 0 for numerical arguments and double
quotes for strings|;
;
;XREAL is used to enter real numbers
(defun XREAL (bit def msg)
    (if  (/= def "")
        (setq msg (strcat "\n" msg " <" (rtos def 2 2) ">  ")
              bit (* (/ bit 2) 2)
        )
        (setq msg (strcat msg ":   "))
    )
    (initget bit)
    (setq val (getreal msg))
    (if (- val nil)
        (setq val def)
    )
)
;
;XINT is used to select integer values
(defun XINT (bit def msg)
    (if (/= dif "")
        (setq msg (strcat "\n" msg " <" (itoa def ) ">  ")
              bit (* (/ bit 2) 2)
        )
        (setq msg (strcat msg ":   "))
    )
    (initget bit)
    (setq val (getint msg))
    (if (- val nil)
        (setq val def)
    )
)
;XKWORD controls string input
(defun XKWORD (bit def kwd msg)
    (if  (/= dif "")
        (setq msg (strcat "\n" msg " <" def  ">  ")
              bit (* (/ bit 2) 2)
        )
        (setq msg (strcat msg ":    "))
    )
```

Continued on the next page

PROGRAM 7.4—(Continued)

```
    )
    (initget bit kwd)
    (setq val (getkword msg))
    (if (= val nil)
        (setq val def)
    )
)
;
;|This function draws a polyline through a set of points and
splines it|;
(defun xpline ( / xpln pnt1 pnt2 )
    (setq xpln xpl
          pnt1  (car xpln)
          pnt2  (cadr xpln)
          xpln  (cdr xpln)
          llim  (getvar "LIMMIN")
          ulim  (getvar "LIMMAX")
    )
;| Sets polyline width to zero and draws first segment through
the first two points of xpln |;
    (command "PLINE" pnt1 "W" 0 0  pnt2 "")
;|Draws remaining segments of polyline by repeatedly stripping
first point from xpl, then drawing polyline through the first two
points in stripped list |;
    (repeat (- npts 2)
        (setq pnt1 (car xpln)
              pnt2 (cadr xpln)
              xpln (cdr xpln)
        )
        (command "PLINE" pnt1 pnt2 "")
    )
;The command function below calls up PEDIT, selects the last entity
drawn (a polyline), then selects everything on the screen and joins
it to the selected polyline.  The resulting polyline is splined
according to the current setting of SPLINETYPE |;
    (command "PEDIT" "L" "J" "C" llim ulim "" "S" "")
) ;Closes xpline
;|Environmental I/O functions.  Lists of variables for old values
and the desired values (A), the names of the system variables (B),
and the number of system variables (NUM) must be externally supplied.
;Extracting current values of system variables
(defun xtract (a b num)
    (repeat num
        (set (car a) (getvar (car b)));|sets AutoLISP variable to
current system variable value|;
        (setq a (cdr a) b (cdr b));|strips first item from each
list|;
    )
)
```

Continued

112

PROGRAM 7.4—(Continued)

```
;|Assignment of values to system variables used at the start of the
program with desired values to reset system variables, and at the
end of the program with the old system variables' values to restore
them.|;
(defun varin ( b a num / x y)
        (repeat num
            (setq a (car a ) b (car b))
            (setvar x y)
            (setq a (cdr a) b (cdr b))
        )
)
;END OF FILE
```

7.6   OVERVIEW OF GRAPH PROGRAM

The program is set up so that the user first specifies the range of the graph. With this data in hand, a scale factor for the point lists may later be determined so that even if the magnitudes of the X and Y coordinates differ widely, they can be plotted to produce a useable curve.

The number of data points and the type of smoothing function to be used are specified next. The user is then prompted to enter each set of data points. The data points are used to produce a list which will first be fed to the PLINE command to produce a line which will be splined. Next, the axes of the graph and tick marks for the major divisions on the axis will be drawn. Finally, a series of POINT commands lay out the data points. Figure 7.1 illustrate the development of XGRAPH.

7.6.1   Data Entry Section

Because the intended users of this program are not acquainted with AutoCAD, many of the data entry prompts will be displayed on the text screen, instead of at the command line. This will allow more explanatory material than could be accommodated in **getxxx** prompts. The initial four items of data needed from the user are (1, 2) the largest X and Y values in the set of data points, (3) the number of data points, and (4) the type of smoothing function. Once these are entered, the programmer can elect to either set up the program environment or input the graph's data points. Both approaches are logical. The former sets the stage for drawing the graph and the latter groups all the user inputs in one section. Let's use the latter approach.

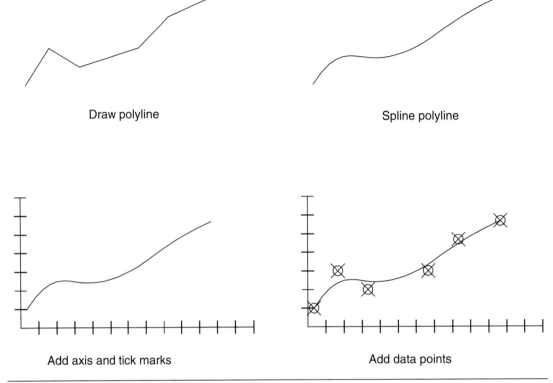

Draw polyline

Spline polyline

Add axis and tick marks

Add data points

FIGURE 7.1   Development of XGRAPH.

Xreal, a user-defined **getreal** function, will be used for the X and Y values. Since the graph is set up in the first quadrant, negative values will be disallowed, and default values will be supplied.

The complete coding for **xreal** is shown below:

```
(defun xreal (bit def msg)
       (if (/= def "")
           (setq msg
                 (strcat "\n" msg "<" (rtos def 2 2)
">: ")
                       bit (* (/ bit 2) 2)
                 )
           (setq msg (strcat "\n" msg ": ")))
       (initget bit)
       (setq val (getreal msg))
       (if (= val nil)
         (setq val def)
         )
         )
```

This coding, of course, would have to be available to the main program, but the main program itself need only include the following:

```
(setq bit 7
      msg "Enter the largest X value"
      def 10
)
(xreal bit def msg)
(setq xval val)
(setq a 7
      b "Enter the largest Y value"
      c 8
)
(xreal a b c)
(setq yval val)
```

and the maximum values would be assigned to *XVAL* and *YVAL* respectively. By the way, *A*, *B*, and *C* in the second section could have been any other three variables (including *BIT*, *MSG*, and *DEF*) as long as they were assigned the appropriate values.

The number of data points will be an integer value. By copying the code for **xreal** and making slight changes you could get the UDF **xint** shown below. (The changes are underlined just to indicate what they are. If you copy the code, omit the underlining.)

```
(defun xint (bit def msg)
      (if (/= def "")
          (setq msg
              (strcat "\n" msg "<" itoa def ">: ")
              bit (* (/ bit 2) 2)
          )
          (setq msg (strcat "\n" msg ": "))
   (initget bit)
   (setq val (getint msg))
   (if (= val nil)
       (setq val def)
   )
 )
```

Again, the UDF code must be available to the program, but inside the program itself, the number of data points could be input by:

```
(setq bit 7 def 10 msg "Number of data points")
(xint bit def msg)
(setq npts val)
```

The final operator input needed to set up the program is the specification of the type of smoothing function. If the operator selects the quadratic function, the system variable SPLINETYPE would be set to 5. If the cubic function is selected, the value would be set to 6.

Of course an **xint**-type function could be used with the operator being told to enter 5 or 6, but it would be more direct to have the operator explicitly choose either "cubic" or "quadratic." When selecting words, rather than numbers, either **getkword** or **getstring** must be used. Since the former gives us better control, let's set up a **getkword** UDF.

The user is presented with a choice of either "Cubic" or "Quadratic" at the prompt line with the default being "Cubic." To make the selection easier for the operator, typing in either "C" or "Q" will make the required selection, but the option of entering the words "quadratic" or "cubic" will also be available for formal lists. The coding for accomplishing this is:

```
(defun xkword (bit def kwd msg)
   (if (and def (/= def ""))
      (progn
          (setq bit (* (/ bit 2) 2)
                msg
                (strcat "\n" msg " <" def ">: ")
          )
       )
          (setq msg (strcat "\n" msg ": "))
   )
   (initget bit kwd)
   (setq val (getkword msg))
   (if (= val nil)
     (setq val def)
   )
)
```

Inside the program, the **xkword** could be called like this:

```
(setq bit 1 def "Cubic" kwd "Cubic Quadratic"
     msg "Cubic or Quadratic fit? (Q/C)"
  )
  (xkword bit def kwd msg)
  (setq type val)
```

If **xkword** were written only for this program, it could be simplified. The programmer, knowing that a default would be supplied, could omit the bitcode as well as the first **if** statement (since the prompt message can include the default). The reason for keeping these tests in the basic UDF is to increase the flexibility of **xkword** so that it can be used in other programs without having to rewrite the function to adapt to changing conditions (e.g., acceptance or rejection of null inputs, presence or absence of defaults). It is this ability to be used under a wide variety of programming conditions that gives user-defined input functions their power. The increase in flexibility more than offsets the increase in the complexity of **xint** and the necessity of entering dummy arguments for any options not used.

Since the programmer doesn't know in advance how many points there will be on the graph, entering these points must be controlled by some type of looping mechanism.

The **while** function, with a flag that would be shut off by the last entry, is one possibility. The **repeat** function is another. Both of these could be programmed to supply prompts that report the number of the point requested so as to minimize user confusion. Input to this section would consist of the number specified by the **xint** function and assigned to the variable *NPTS* and a set of point lists. The output—a list of point lists—would be used to plot the data points and draw the PLINE that will represent the data curve.

The program will ask the user to select points using the **getpoint** function (which will accept either screen or keyboard input) and add the points to a list with **cons**. A counter will be embodied in the prompt to tell the user which point is being entered. An **initget** with a bitcode of 1 disallowing null input will be used to filter out improper inputs. All Z coordinates will be set to zero. The prompt for the last input will differ from those for the preceding inputs so the **getpoint** prompt will have to be changed. This could be handled with an **if** function, but then the function would have to be evaluated for every entry. A better alternative is to repeat the entry procedure n − 1 times, then input the last entry outside the loop.

If the programmer frequently has to construct lists, the coding for the data point entry could be embodied in a UDF. For the present, it is presented as part of the main program.

```
(setq xnum (1- npts)
    count 1
)
(repeat xnum
    (initget 1)
    (setq msg (strcat
    "\nPick or key in point " (itoa count) ": "
"
                    );close strcat
        ptn (getpoint msg)
        ptn (list (car ptn) (cadr ptn) 0)
        xpl (cons ptn xpl)
       count (1+ count)
    );setq
);end of repeat loop
    (initget 1)
    (setq msg "\nPick or key in last point: "
        ptn (getpoint msg)
        ptn (list (car ptn) (cadr ptn) 0)

        xpl (cons ptn xpl)
    );setq
```

7.6.2 Data Manipulation

Since it is undesirable to plot quantities of widely differing magnitudes on linear plots (e. g., hundreds of watts against fractions of amperes), a check should be made to see that the maximum X and Y values are on the same order of magnitude, and if not, to multiply the smaller value by a suitable scale factor. The scale factor could be found by:

```
(setq xscale 1 yscale 1 a xval b yval )
      (if (> b a)
         (setq flag 1);Y value is largest
      )
      (setq ratio (/ b a ))
      (if (= flag 1)
        (setq yscale
           (atof (rtos (/ 1 ratio) 2 1))
        )
        (setq xscale (atof (rtos ratio 2 1)))
      )
```

At this point you know that the maximum values of X and Y on the graph will be (* xval xscale) and (* yval yscale). You could use these values to establish the lengths of the axes. However, from an aesthetic standpoint, it is desirable to make the axes a little larger. This can be accomplished by redefining *XVAL* and *YVAL* as equal to 110% of their scaled former values.

```
(setq xval (* 1.1 xval xscale)
      yval (* 1.1 yval yscale)
)
```

By redefining existing variables instead of introducing a new set of variables, you conserve the memory space allocated to holding the values of AutoLISP variables. It also simplifies the subsequent coding and makes it easier to understand. Using the new variables, you can establish the points necessary for drawing the X and Y axes as well as the spacing for the tick marks on these axes:

```
(setq ul (list 0 yval )
      lr (list xval 0)
   xdist (/ xval 10)
   ydist (/ yval 10)
)
```

Later, you'll draw lines from *UL* down to 0,0 and then right to *LR*. These lines will form, respectively, the Y and X axes of the graph.

7.6.3   The Environment Modules

The environment requirements of this program are minimal. You will have to set the limits of the drawing before actually drawing the graph, the size and type of the POINT entity must be set, and the value of SPLINETYPE must be set to create the type of curve specified by the string assigned to *TYPE*. The system variables involved will be LIM-MIN and LIMMAX to set the limits, PDSIZE and PDMODE for POINT size and appearance, and SPLINETYPE. The last setting is slightly complicated by the fact that the value for *TYPE* (either "Cubic" or "Quadratic") must be converted to either 6 or 5, since SPLINETYPE accepts only numerical values. The coding below will handle the conversion:

```
(if (= type "quadratic")
        (setq type 5)
        (setq type 6)
)
```

but since we will be using *TYPE* to designate the value of SPLINETYPE rather than the actual value, the list of desired values must be constructed using **list**, rather than **quote**.

As usual, we will have to capture the present values of each of these variables, reset them to the desired values, then return the initial values when exiting the graphing program. Table 7.4 summarizes the requirements.

The procedure and programs for handling system variables were discussed earlier in the chapter, but will be summarized here. Lists of the five system variables to be modified, the variables to represent their current values, and their desired values will be made up either by using **setq** and **quote** or **list** functions outside the subprogram, or by using a UDF-embodying procedure similar to those used to enter the data points. The first two lists will be supplied to **xtract**, which will use **getvar** to assign the current values to the variables in the second column of the table above. Then the list of system variables and

TABLE 7.4   System Variable Requirements for XGRAPH

System Variable Function and Name	Variable Name	Desired Value
Upper right drawing limit LIMMAX	*oul*	(list (car lr) (cadr ul))
Lower left drawing limit LIMMIN	*oll*	'(0 0)
Size of POINT PDSIZE	*ops*	5 (5% of screen size)
Type of Point PDMODE	*opm*	2 (plus sign)
Curve fitting function SPLINETYPE	*ost*	5/6 (quadratic/cubic)

the list of desired values will be submitted to **varin,** which will use **setvar** to set the system variables to their new values. Before exiting the program, **varin** will be used again to reset the system variables to their former values.

7.6.4   Accessing the Drawing

This portion of the program will first set the drawing limits using the values of LIMMIN and LIMMAX. This will be followed by two ZOOM commands, first a ZOOM All, then a ZOOM .9X to improve the appearance of the final drawing. A **repeat** loop will be used to draw a PLINE between each pair of data points.[5] Using PEDIT, the polyline segments will first be joined then splined to form the data curve.

The PEDIT command selects everything on the screen to be joined to the polyline, so neither the data points nor the axes can be created before the polyline is edited. With PEDIT completed, the LINE command is used to draw the two axes, and a plus-mark-type POINT is placed on each axis at one-tenth of the distance from the origin to the end of the axis. Finally, two ARRAY commands are used to generate ten evenly spaced copies of each point. The axes will cover two of the four lines constituting the point, and the remaining two lines will serve as tick marks that can be subsequently labeled with values.

The last step in drawing the graph is to place a POINT at each of the data points. If desired, PDMODE could be changed at this point, so that a different type of POINT could be used to represent the data points on the screen.[6]

Because this program is complex and may require extensive trouble shooting, UDFs were created to draw and spline the polyline, draw the axes and tick marks, and place POINTS on the data points. While these UDFs will probably not be used in subsequent programs, using them to debug this program eliminated a lot of repetitious data entry.

The complete graphing program, along with the associated UDFs, is shown in Program 7.4 (pages 107–113). As you can see, the UDFs embody most of the complexities involved with the program. By using existing UDFs, a great deal of programming was eliminated. The few new UDFs that were created more than paid for

---

[5]Since *XPL*, the list of data points, will be used both to draw the PLINE segments and to place POINTS at the data points, it cannot be altered by the procedures used to draw the polyline. If *XPL* is redefined as a new variable, the new variable can be used to draw the polylines, leaving *XPL* itself for laying down the POINTS.

[6]Since PLOT automatically causes a REGEN (which sets all entities to the current values of the system variables), PDMODE must remain set at 2 if hard copies of the graph are desired or the tick marks on the axes will not be properly presented.

themselves when the program was being debugged, even though they probably will never be used in other programs.

Program 7.4 illustrates a number of points. By declaring the variables used in **xgraph** as local, the memory space used by these variables is released upon exiting the program. Additional variables, such as X and Y in **varin**, are used only as placeholders and are declared local by the subfunctions that use them. Since the program is complex, there are a lot of variables involved—an alphabetical list helps keep track of them. In addition, a complete list of all the variables used and their function in the program could be appended to the program as a comment.

The variable list was reduced even further by reusing many of the variables in the UDFs. **Bit**, **def**, **kwd**, and **msg** are common to many data-entry UDFs. They can be used outside their UDFs to assign values as well as inside UDFs to control input. Consistency not only saves memory space, it also helps avoid mistakes, for instance by assigning "Enter a number" as a bit code for an **initget**. Keeping arguments in alphabetical order in function variable lists also helps to ensure that correct values are assigned to each argument within the function.

While it is a good idea to keep a list of the variables used while you're in the process of writing the program, leave them undeclared until the programming is complete and the resulting code is debugged. Neither local variables nor global arguments used as locals within a subprogram will retain the values they had if the subprogram crashes. By using **setq**s to define global values before the subprogram is called, and by not declaring variables used only within the program as local, their current values will be available if the program crashes. While debugging a failed program is never easy, knowing variables' values at the time of the crash helps in isolating the cause of the failure.

Since the intent of the program is to draw graphs for relatively untrained users, prompting and explanatory material must be expanded. By using **textpage** to flip to the text screen, the program gave the user a chance to read and assimilate the background material. A line of **prompt**s followed by the **princ** function printed out detailed instructions to the user, followed by a blank line. A dummy data entry function using **getstring** prompted the user to hit any key to move to the next step. When the function was satisfied by hitting any key and a return, either **graphscr** or **textpage** brought up the drawing screen or cleared the text screen for additional instructions. The variable that the dummy entry was assigned to was redefined and used for another purpose later in the program, thus preventing the list of local variables from growing even larger.

One final note. When **xgraph** was writted, there wasn't a program available for creating a list of points. After writing the code for getting the points in the main portion of **xgraph**, it seemed like a good idea to create such a function. By bringing up **xgraph** on a word processor and copying the code in question to another ASCII file, a new UDF could be created without even having to retype the code. The lesson? Programs can be used to produce UDFs, just as UDFs can be used to create progams. The newly created function is shown as Program 7.5. It can be substituted for the equivalent coding in **xgraph**.

PROGRAM 7.5—MAKING A LIST OF POINTS

```
;|"This function allows the user to select a number of points
previously specified by the variable NPTS. Hitting the return
key at the prompt is disallowed by setting an initget bit value
to 1. Z coordinates of points are set to zero so that the graph
may be drawn with 2-D polylines. |;
;(defun C:GETPT ( / ptn count xnum)
    (setq  xnum (1- npts)
         count 1
    )
    (repeat xnum
       (initget 1)
       (setq msg
           (strcat "\nPick or key in point "(itoa count))
             ptn (getpoint msg);selects point
;                   Z coordinate of supplied point forced to  0
            ptn (list (car ptn) (cadr ptn) 0);
            xpl (cons ptn xpl); point added to list
           count (1+ count);counter incremented
         )
;|The coding above handles inputting of all but the last point.
The prompt for entering the point should be changed to inform the
user that the last point in the sequence is about to be entered|;
        (initget 1);forces input
        (setq msg "\nPick or key in last point:   "
             ptn  (getpoint msg)
             ptn  (list (car ptn) (cadr ptn) 0)
             xpl  (cons ptn xpl)
       );closes setq
);closes function
```

EXERCISES

These exercises all involve writing programs. In each case, write a program complete with prompts and environment sections. If you haven't done so already, try setting up UDFs, particularly for the input and environment sections. You may stipulate any additional conditions or limitations you feel necessary for the program to function, but you'll have to live with the stipulated conditions in each exercise.

1. Dimensioning a view is difficult if the corners have been broken with fillets or chamfers, because neither the original endpoints nor the initial lines are available for selection at the dimension prompt. Write a program that will automatically dimension a filleted or chamfered line, showing the initial, rather than the shortened, length of the line.

2. Electromechanical controls frequently use a ladder diagram to show a symbolic representation of the interconnection of the control elements. The diagram (see Figure 7.2) consists of pairs of vertical lines connected with horizontal "rungs." Symbols, representing control components such as contacts, solenoids, push buttons, and limit switches, are placed on the rungs to show the system's logic.

Assume that you have a library of such components, each drawn as a block within a 0.5 unit square, with the insertion point on the line representing the left end of the component and an attribute to serve as a label. You also have a partial ladder diagram, consisting of two vertical lines and a number of horizontal rungs.

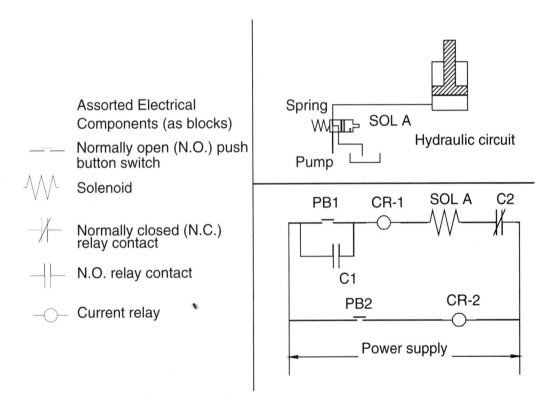

Operation of circuit: Pushing PB1 powers CR-1, SOL A, and C1. SOL A switches valve, ram extends, contact C1 keeps relay on after push button is released. PB2 powers CR-2 which opens relay C2, cutting off power to CR-1 and SOL A. Spring returns valve to initial position, allowing hydraulic fluid to drain to tank.

FIGURE 7.2 Simple Ladder Diagram.

Write a program that will allow the operator to insert a specified component. The program should break out a 0.5-unit-long section of the rung at a specified point, insert the block representing the component, and allow the operator to specify the component's label.

3. Write a program to draw a slot at a specified location. The slot is formed by two 180° arcs connected by lines. The user will input the center of the left arc, the angle of the slot, the length of the slot, and the width.

4. Write a program similar to Exercise 3 that will draw a slot consisting of two 180° arcs connected by two larger arcs. Give the user the choice of specifying the centerline of the slot with a three-point arc or by specifying the center of the first end arc in the CCW direction, the center of the larger arcs, and the chord length of the centerline arc. Give the user the option of entering the slot's width on the screen or from the keyboard.

CHAPTER 8

Accessing the Database

OBJECTIVES

After reading this chapter, you will be able to:

- Use entity data lists to access a drawing's database.
- Extract data lists for an entity.
- Change the characteristics (e.g., size, linetype, layer) of selected entities by accessing the database with an AutoLISP program.

8.1   ENTITY DATA LISTS

While many AutoLISP programs work effectively by feeding data to AutoCAD commands, there are times when it is more efficient to short circuit the process by having AutoLISP work directly on the drawing's database instead of indirectly through the **command** function. To make use of such access, it is necessary to understand how the AutoCAD database works.

Every entity on a drawing has a name which is unique to the entity and which is assigned for the duration of the drawing session.[1] Using the entity's name, the user may

---

[1]Actually a second name, called a handle, can be assigned at the option of the operator. Handles are also unique to the entity, but unlike names, they retain their identities even after exiting the drawing editor.

access the database entries for that entity, and, if necessary, modify them. The database entries for an entity take the form of a list, such as the one shown below:

```
((-1. <Entity Name 60000C16>)(0 . "CIRCLE")(8 . "X5")
(10 7.87 6.00 0.00)(40 . 0.125)(210 0.0 0.0 1.0))
```

The list consists of a mixture of conventional lists and dotted pairs. A dotted pair is a list consisting of two atoms separated by a period with leading and trailing spaces. (That's why real numbers cannot start or end with a decimal point—if they did, AutoLISP would treat them as if they were part of a dotted pair.) They can be constructed by using **cons** with two-atom arguments instead of an atom and a list. The most important thing that distinguishes dotted pairs from normal two-atom lists is that the **cdr** of a dotted pair is *not* a list while the **cdr** of a normal list is *always* a list.

The **car** of each dotted pair or conventional sublist in the data list is known as the group code, and tells the knowledgeable operator what property of the entity is represented by the sublist. The group code meanings for a few entities are given in Table 8.1. Items in quotes are string values, the unquoted values starting with uppercase letters are real numbers, and the codes starting with lowercase letters are integers.

Table 8.1 shows the major codes for some of AutoCAD's primitive entities. Additional codes are included if linetypes and colors are not by layer (6 and 62), if the thickness is not zero (39), and if the Z coordinate of an entity's extrusion direction is not parallel to the World Coordinate System's Z axis (210). In general, these additional group codes are included only if the values in question are not the defaults and are nonzero. The codes for the other entities are similar to the ones listed in the table. Some codes are common to all entities. On the other hand, additional codes are used to represent unique characteristics of each type of entity, such as the invisibility status of 3-D faces, the starting and ending angles of arcs, the definition points of dimensions, and the like.

By using these codes and referring to the data list cited earlier in the chapter, we can tell that the entity in question is named 60000C16 (group code –1), and that it is a circle (code 0), with a radius of 0.125 (code 40), centered at 7.87, 6, 0 (code 10) on layer X5 (code 8). Since the extrusion direction of the entity was on the WCS Z axis, the circle must have been drawn on, or parallel to, the WCS's X–Y plane.

Although the coding may appear complex, it is relatively simple to decipher, particularly if the appropriate AutoCAD manuals are available.[2] If information about a particular

---

[2]Those trying to develop a systematic understanding of data lists by consulting the AutoCAD manuals or other texts should be aware of the fact that most discussions of data list coding are based on DXF entity codes. There are some differences. The *AutoCAD V. 11 Reference Manual*, for instance, states that Groups 10, 20, and 30 are the X, Y, and Z coordinates of lines' starting points, and Groups 11, 21, and 31 are the coordinates of the endpoints. In data lists, the starting points of lines are shown as a four-member conventional (i.e., *nondotted pair*) list of the form (10 2.0 3.5 0.0) and endpoints are represented by data lists with an 11 code. A partial coverage of entity group codes may be found in *AutoCAD Release 12 LISP Reference* (Autodesk Publication #102349), pp. 120–123. *AutoCAD Release 12 Advanced Tools* (Autodesk publication 102351) covers group codes from the DXF standpoint on pp. 281–303.

TABLE 8.1 Reading the Database

Code	Line	Arc	Text
−1		"Entity Name"	
0		"Entity Type"	
1	–	–	"Text Value"
5		"Handle"	
7			"Text Style Name"
8		"Layer"	
10	Start Coordinate	Center	Insertion Point
11	End Coordinate	–	Alignment Point
40	–	Radius	Text Height
41			X Scale Factor
50	–	Start Angle	–
51		End Angle	Insert Angle
71	–	–	generation flag*
72	–	–	h. justification
73	–	–	v. justification

*2 if text is backward, 4 if upside down, 6 if both.

type of entity is needed on the fly, the easiest way to get it is to put a few samples of that entity on a scratch drawing, access their data lists using the **entsel** and **entget** functions discussed below, and determine what the unknown group codes represent by comparing the different entities. (Be aware that data lists for polylines of more than one or two segments tend to be very long.)

8.2 EXTRACTING DATA LISTS

Viewing the data list of an entity is a two-step process. First the *name* of the entity is obtained then, using the entity's name, the corresponding data list is called up. In data processing terms, an entity's name is a pointer, enabling the computer to locate the record of that entity in the database file.

TABLE 8.2   Entity Selection and Modification Functions

Function	Notes
(entdel (name))	Deletes entities in the drawing, *un*deletes entities that have previously been deleted.
(entget (name))	Supplies data list for specified entity.
(entlast)	Returns name of last nondeleted entry in data list. Used with **entnext** to get newest entry.
(entmake (elist))	Creates new entity corresponding to *elist.*
(entmod (elist))	Updates main entities in *elist* after data list is altered. See **entupd** below.
(entnext [name])	Returns name of entity *following* name. If name omitted, returns first nondeleted entity in database.
(entsel [prompt])	Returns entity name and selection point. Use **car** to pull out entity name.
(entupd (name))	Updates modified subentities (e.g., Attributes, Polyline vertices). Analogous to **entmod.**
(handent (handle))	Returns entity name associated with handle.
(ssget)	Builds selection set using standard selection modes in "Select object(s)" format. Highlights selected entities.
(ssget "opt")	Builds selection set using specified format. "Opt" may be any selection mode (e.g., P, W, C, L, etc.). Option must be in quotes. See discussion of "X" option below.
(ssget ["opt"] (pts))	Same as above, except selection point(s) are specified by lists of coordinates.
(sslength (ss))	Returns number of items in selection set.
(ssmem (name ss))	Returns entity name if it is in the selection set, otherwise returns "nil."
(ssname ss index)	Returns entity names of members of set in order (index starts with 0).

There are two types of functions that deal with entities' names: the **entxxx** functions and the **ssget** functions. The former deals with the entities one at a time; the latter builds a selection set that can contain any number of entity names. The only function that actually calls up an entity's data list is the **entget** function, which is discussed below, along with the other entity handling and selection functions.

In Table 8.2, which lists the entity selection functions, NAME refers to the entity name, the **cdr** of the 0. group; ELIST is a set of one or more entity names; the permanent identifier of an entity (accessible as the **cdr** of the 5. group); and (ss) is a selection set consisting of one or more entities. Optional terms are indicated by brackets [].

One function, **ssget**, merits special discussion. If **ssget** is used with the "X" option and a list of filters, it will cull the entire database and select only those entities that match the filter requirements. For example:

```
(ssget "X" '((0."LINE")(8."CENTER")))
```

will return a list of the names of all lines on the "CENTER" layer. The selection process may be further modified by using the relational or logical operation listed in Table 8.3 to construct filter lists to narrow the selection criteria.

The filter list, which must be an AutoLISP quoted list, may be modified by using relational or logical operators as dotted pairs preceded by a –4 group code. These operators could, for example, scan the database and select all entities which are circles *and* have a radius greater than 0.25 by using a filter list such as:

```
'(
      ( -4 . "<AND" )
              (0 . "CIRCLE")
          (-4 . ">") (40 . 0.25)
      (-4 . "AND>")
  )
```

Notice how all the operators and operands are grouped within a single quoted list. This is one instance where **quote** or its alias, ', must be used instead of the **list** function. The latter would attempt to evaluate the list instead of just feeding it to the **ssxxx** function.

If the 40 group code were only associated with circles, it wouldn't have been necessary to include the (0 . "CIRCLE") filter in the list. Unfortunately, many other entities use the 40 code in their entity lists, so it's best to include an entity filter (i.e., a 0 group) in all such lists.

Below is a more complex filter list. Try to decipher what the list is calling for before you read the explanation that follows it.

```
'( (-4 . "<AND")
                  (-4 . <OR)
                    (0 . "CIRCLE")
                    (0 . "ARC")
                        (-4 . "OR>")
                        (-4 . "<OR")
                            (40 . 0.5)
                    (8 . "CONSTRUCT")
                        (-4 . "OR>")
                  (-4 . "AND>")
      )
  )
```

TABLE 8.3 Relational and Logical Operators for SSXXX Functions

Operator	Type	Notes
"*"	Logical	Any value (always true)
"="	Logical	Not equal
"!="	Logical	Not equal
"<>"	Logical	Not equal
"<"	Logical	Less than
"<="	Logical	Less than or equal
">"	Logical	Greater than
">="	Logical	Greater than or equal
"&"	Logical	Bitwise AND (integers only)
"&="	Logical	Bitwise masked equals (integers only)
"<AND"/"AND>"	Relative	Tests two or more operands
"<OR"/"OR>"	Relative	Tests two or more operands
"<XOR"/"XOR>"	Relative	Compares two operands
"<NOT"/"NOT>"	Relative	Negates one operand

Note: Logical operators are quoted and used in pairs before and after the operands, with < in front of the starting operator and > following the ending operator. Relational operators are used singly within double quotes. Both types are preceded by a –4 group code and form the **cdr** of a dotted pair, e.g., (–4 . "<AND") operands (–4 . "AND>"), or (–4 . "=").

This list, when used with an **ssxxx** function, will return a set of the names of all entities which are either circles *or* arcs *and* either have radii equal to 0.5 *or* are on layer "Construct".

Since **ssget** when used with the "X" option and a filter list searches the entire database, it will catch entities that are off the screen or that are on frozen or turned-off layers. This could be either an advantage or a disadvantage, depending on the desired nature of the selection set.

As mentioned above, **entxxx** functions select one entity at a time and return only the name of that entity (with the exception of **entsel**, which also returns the coordinates of the point used to select the entity). Once the entity name is available, it is submitted to **entget** which returns the data list. The data list may be obtained in either a one- or a two-step process.

```
(setq a (entlast) ;sets a to the name of the last
                  ;nondeleted entity in the database
```

```
            b (entget a); returns the entity list
)
```

The alternative one step-process will produce the same result, but will save typing:

```
(setq b (entget (entlast)))
```

It isn't necessary to use **entlast** for this process; almost any **ent** function could be used.

Entsel is very useful in selecting individual entities, but since it returns both the entity name and the pick point in the form:

```
(<Entity name: 60000123> (1.0 2.0 3.0))
```

only the **car** may be submitted to **entget** when an entity name is required.

The best approach to using **ssxxx** functions is to use **sslength** to establish the number of items in the selection set. Then, using **ssname**'s index, step through the set item by item as shown below:

```
    (setq a (ssget "W"); uses a window for selection
          i (sslength a);number of items in selection set
          num 0; initializes counter
    )
    (while (< num i)
        (setq b (entget (ssname a num));|returns name of
first member of set|;
                    .
                    .ADDITIONAL COMMANDS
                    .
                (setq i (1+ num);increments num
    );closes while
```

The fragment shown will supply the name of each member of Selection Set A in sequence. Any form of screen selection may be used to establish the initial selection set by replacing the "W" with another option or omitting it completely (in which case a "Select object(s) prompt will be issued, just as it is in AutoCAD).

8.3   USING ENTITY LISTS TO REPLACE SCREEN PICKS

Using the database as an alternative to screen picks enables the programmer to simplify the program, since screen input is minimized, reducing the need to protect against entry mistakes. Consider, for example, the program to write the diameters and centers of circles to a file. That program required the user to make a pair of picks for each circle, and an additional pair to exit. Using the database, the circle's centers and diameters could be written to a file with the CIRCDAT2 program (Program 8.1.)

Once you clearly understand the relationship between the entity's name (*ENTN* in the CIRCDAT2 program), and the entity's data list (*EL* in the program), the programming is relatively straightforward. Select all the circles in the drawing to create selection set (*SS*), get *NUM* (the number of atoms in the set), and go through the loop *NUM* times. Within the loop use **ssname** and an index to extract *ENTN* (the entity's name) and **entget** to assign the entity's data list (*EL*). Once the data list is accessible, use **assoc** and the various list extraction functions to get *DX*, *DY*, and *DIA*[3] from the appropriate code groups.

PROGRAM 8.1—AUTOMATED DATA EXTRACTION (CIRCDAT2)

```
;|This program replicates the results of CIRCDATA in Chapter 6.
Since ssxxx functions are not affected by Osnaps, unless they are
declared within the function, the environment setting and
resetting sections are unnecessary|;

(defun C:CIRCDAT2  ()
    (setq out (open "CIRCLES.TXT" "w")
           ss (ssget "X" '(( 0 . "CIRCLE")));selects circles
           num (sslength ss);number of circles in database
    )
;     Print up heading
    (princ "NUMBER\nDIAMETER\nX-COORD\nYCOORD" out)
    (repeat num ;loops once for each circle
        (setq ssi (- num 1);ssname index starts at 0
              entn (ssname el ssi);name of entity
               el (entget entn);entity list
             cord (assoc 10 el);center of entity
               dx (rtos (cadr cord));X coordinate
               dy (rtos (caddr cord));Y coordinate
              dia (rtos (* 2 (cdr (assoc 40 el)))));diameter
        );closes setq
        (write-line (rtos num) out);writes the item number to file
        (write-line dia out);writes diameter to file
        (write-line dx out);writes X coord. to file
        (write-line dy out);writes Y coord. to file
        (princ  "\n" out);blank line for spacing
    );closes repeat loop
    (close out)
    (princ)
);end of function
```

---

[3] Since the entity list for a circle returns the radius of the circle as the CDR of the group 40 code, you'll have to double it to get the diameter.

From both the user's and programmmer's standpoints, the CIRCDAT2 program is an improvement over CIRCDATA: Once CIRCDAT2 former is invoked, it extracts the necessary data without any additional operator input. This means that the program will be easier to use and justify.

Another interesting, although impractical, demonstration of the possibilities available through database access is automated dimensioning—a procedure for dimensioning the exterior lines in any view of a given object. This procedure requires that all of these lines must be drawn in one direction, either clockwise or anticlockwise (although they need not be drawn in succession). If this condition is met, Program 8.2 will completely dimension the linear exterior features of the object.

PROGRAM 8.2—AUTOMATED DIMENSIONING

```
(defun C:AUTDIM ()
   (setq set (ssget "W"); builds selection set
         len (sslength set);number of entities in set
         msg "\nDimension line offset distance:  "
           d  (getpoint msg)
      index 1;counter
    )
    (repeat len
       (setq  ent (ssname set index);selects entity
              dlst  (entget (car (entsel)));data list
                pt1 (xpt dlst 3);UDF to get start point
                pt2 (xpt dlst 4); end point
                ang  (angle pt1 pt2);angle of line
                ang  (+ (/ pi 2) ang);adds 90 degrees
                pt3  (xmid pt1 pt2)
                pt4  (polar pt3 ang d);offset point
              index   (1+ index);updates count
       )
       (command "DIM" "ALI" "" pt3  pt4 "")
    );close repeat
);close function
;|Below are two UDFs written for this program, xpt extracts the
value of an endpoint from the fourth (10 group) or fifth (11
group) of a line's data list (starting from 0).  Xmid locates a
point midway between the entity's endpoints. |;
(defun xpt (a b)
;a is the data list, b is 3 (for 10 group) or 4 (for 11 group)
      (list (cadr (nth a b))(caddr (nth a b)))
);closes xpt
(defun xmid (a b);a and b are two point lists
      (list
        (/ (+ (car a)(car b)) 2)(/ (+ (cadr a)(cadr b)) 2)
      )
  )
```

The program is really an extension of XDIM (Program 4.3), which selected a vertical, horizontal, or aligned dimension for a given line. In this case, all the exterior lines are selected with an **ssget** function to form a selection set. The name of each member of this set is selected in turn with an **ssname** function, and the line's definition data are assigned to a variable with **entget** and **car** of **entsel**. The **cadr** and **caddr** of the 10 and 11 group codes[4] are used to obtain the coordinates of the line's endpoints. Next, the angle from the starting endpoint to the other end is obtained with the **angle** function. The midpoint of the line indicates the line being dimensioned (using AutoCAD's ". . . RETURN to select:" option). The "Dimension line location" prompt is satisfied by using **polar** to set a point at a preset distance at an angle 90 degrees greater than the angle between the start and endpoints (or 90 degrees less, if the line is drawn in the anticlockwise direction). With this information in hand, the program can either determine the type of dimension line or (for simplicity's sake) simply use aligned dimensions and take the default dimension value. When the first line in the selection set is dimensioned, **ssname** brings up the next member of the set, and the process is repeated. The coding for the program assumes the outline to be drawn clockwise and that only exterior lines are selected with **ssget**, so no attempt is made to filter out other entities.

Since this program doesn't allow for baseline dimensioning or leave space for dimensioning interior features, it isn't really too effective in the real world.

8.4   CHANGING ENTITIES BY MODIFICATION OF ENTITY LISTS

Building lists and executing AutoCAD commands are not the only tasks where access to the database can be used. Suppose that a previously created drawing entity is changed by editing it. What will happen to that entity's data list? If a circle's radius is increased from 0.125 to 0.1875, for example, the **cdr** of the 40 group will also change to 0.1875; there is a one-to-one relationship between an entity and its data list. This being the case, it is possible to alter the data list and have the change reflected in the entity. This is not to say that it makes sense to abandon the MOVE, CHANGE, and CHPROP commands in favor of database manipulation whenever we have to edit a drawing. Most of the time, entity modification is better done on the graphics screen instead of with an entity list. There are, however, some exceptions.

Returning, once again, to the part with a large number of holes of varying diameters in it, let's suppose that because of a redesign, the specification for all the 0.25 diameter

---

[4]The 10 group gives the starting point and the 11 group the endpoint in LINE data lists. Unlike most of the other groups in a data list, the 10 and 11 data are in a conventional list, not a dotted pair.

holes is increased to 0.3125 without changing their locations. This change, involving a large number of items, is a good candidate for the entity list approach. The first step is to build up a selection set consisting of all entities on the drawing with a group code 0 value of "CIRCLE", and a 0.125 value for group code 40. This can be done with **ssget**, as follows:

```
(setq ss (ssget "X" '(( 0 . "CIRCLE")(40 . 0.125))))
```

Then extract the entity list for each entity in turn. Be sure to put a space before and after the period in the sublists.

The change is accomplished in two steps. First, a 40 . 0.15625 dotted pair is created, then it is substituted for the current 40 . 0.125 pair. Since both pairs may be treated as strings, the **substr** function is used. Assuming that the entity list is assigned to *EL*, the coding would look like this:

```
(setq el (subst;substitute
         (cons 40 0.15625);new setting
         (assoc 40 el); for old setting
          el); in list el
);end setq
```

The same approach could be used to initiate less specific changes. Suppose an architectural drawing is to be plotted to a small "B" size sheet instead of the "E" size sheet it was created for. The dimensions could all be changed by resetting the appropriate controls and doing an UPDATE from the dimension prompt, but the operator would have to select each text item and use the CHANGE command on it. This type of situation is a good candidate for the database approach.

Let's assume that it has been decided that the minimum size text on the old drawing that would be readable on the reduced drawing is 0.375. Any text smaller than this would have to be increased to 0.375, but any larger text would be unchanged. This rules out using something like:

```
'((0 . "TEXT")(40 . 0.1875))
```

as the filter list, since it would select text entities with a height of 0.1875 but not other small sizes. This is where relational operators earn their keep. A list such as:

```
'(    (-4 . "<AND")
          (0 . "TEXT")
      (-4 . "<")
             (40 . 0.375)
          (-4 . "AND>")
)
```

would produce a selection set containing *only* text with heights less than 0.375. This list could be fed to a **substr** function to replace the entity's old group 40 sublists with (40 . 0.375), thus producing an entity list that will reflect the desired state of affairs.

But changing the entity list does not, of itself, change the entity's image on the screen. That's a job for the **entmod** function, which updates the entity after all the entity list changes have been made. For the current problem, all that is necessary is to include the line:

```
(entmod el)
```

in the program code following all coding for the substitutions, and the screen images of the entities will be updated.

There are a number of restrictions associated with **entmod**. To start with, if you change a linetypes, text style, or block reference, the new linetype, text style, or block must already exist on the drawing. (**Entmod** will, however, create a new layer.) In addition, **entmod** will not redisplay complex entities such as polylines and blocks with attributes; another function, **entupd**, is required for that. (Even using **entupd** does not guarantee an updated image on the screen. In some instances, the AutoCAD REGEN command must be invoked.) Finally, while **entmod** can be used to replace Block "A" with Block "B," if it is used in an attempt to change entities *within* a block definition it will cause AutoCAD to crash.

Considering the effort required to program changes in complex entities such as polylines and blocks—and the possible risks of degrading the database—it probably is better to change these types of entities with AutoCAD commands from the screen instead of using AutoLISP programs. The same reasoning applies to using the **entmake** function to draw an object on the screen. It can be done, but it isn't really worth the effort. On the other hand, it does make sense to go to the data list for data extraction, such as with CIRCDAT2. The database approach may even be used for entity evaluation. The programs in Chapter 4, which required a list of circle's centers and diameters (Exercises 4 and 5), could also have used the database approach.

EXERCISES

Since this is the last chapter, use all the bells and whistles you can within each program. Be sure to use good prompts, since the average user isn't acquainted with database handling techniques. You might want to *make* an opportunity for user input. For instance, in Exercise 1, you could let the user select a color for each size circle instead of having the computer do it for them. There are many people around who get nervous at the thought of putting control in the hands of a computer. By giving them an opportunity to exercise such control, even when it isn't necessary, you might make your programs more acceptable to users.

1. A plate has a number of holes in it. The holes range in diameter from 0.5 to 0.9 units in 0.1-unit increments. Using database access techniques, change the colors of the holes so that holes of each diameter have a unique color.

2. If the default for a dimension is overridden, the data list for DIMENSION entities shows the value of the dimension in the Group Code 1 sublist. Assume that a drawing produced by an individual who overrode all the linear dimensions must have all "1.25" long lines changed to "1.27" (even though the lines are not 1.27 long). Write a program to access the database and make the required change.

3. The restriction that all lines be drawn in the same direction limits the use of the **autdim** program by restricting the way the operator can use AutoCAD. If, however, the outline is converted to a single polyline and later exploded, a set of LINE entities will be produced. All the lines in this set will be drawn in either the clockwise or anticlockwise direction, so once the direction is determined for one line, **autdim** may be applied. Using conventional AutoCAD techniques, draw a closed figure with both clockwise and anticlockwise lines, then convert the lines to a single polyline using PEDIT to convert the first line and join it to the rest. (An alternative approach would be to use BPOLY to produce a polyline on top of the initial figure.[5]) When the polyline is exploded, all the line entities will either go clockwise or anticlockwise. Write an AutoLISP program that will determine if the lines run clockwise, supply the appropriate response to the "Dimension line location:" prompt, and dimension the figure.

---

[5]BPOLY is not an AutoCAD command in the sense that LINE, ERASE, or LIST is. Code for these commands is embedded in the basic AutoCAD program. On the other hand, when BPOLY is entered at the command line, an AutoLISP program of the same name is accessed. In AutoCAD, this makes no difference to the user, but in AutoLISP the distinction means that BPOLY cannot be accessed with the **command** function, but must be called up, just as if it were a UDF, that is, with (BPOLY).

APPENDIX A

Syntax of AutoLISP Functions

As is the case with other computer languages, AutoLISP functions require the programmer to satisfy syntax requirements. The listing below is intended to provide a definitive guide to the syntax of all AutoLISP functions in AutoCAD version 12. However, no guide can cover all the nuances of all the available functions, so it is best to look on this listing as a starting point rather than the solution to all syntax problems.

This listing is a modified version of the listing in *AutoCAD Release 12: AutoLISP Reference,* Autodesk Inc., Publication 102349, June 28, 1993. It is used with the permission of the copyright holder, AutoDESK Inc.

To make the definitions more uniform, most of the elements required by the listed functions are shown in Table A.1. Where necessary, specific requirements for each function are included in the function's listing. All the items in the listing for a given function are required to be present, except for those enclosed in brackets [ ]. In some cases, a given element may optionally be present more than once. This situation is indicated by the presence of ellipses (. . .) after the term in question. An asterisk (*) after an element in a listing indicates the existence of a special condition, which is covered in a note at the end of the discussion of that function.

Arithmetic symbols

(sym v/v [v/v . . .]*)

sym   One of the following: +, -, *, or /
v/v   Must represent numerical quantities. If any variables are real, the function will return a real.

TABLE A.1   Abbreviations Used in AutoLISP Function Definitions

Abbreviation	Notes
a/l	Atom or list
atm	Atom—any AutoLISP quantity *except* a list
elst	Entity data list
enam	Entity name, the **cdr** of the −1 group
expr	Expression—a logical or arithmetical relationship between two or more atoms, or lists that may contain numbers, strings, or the variables representing them
fl	Flag—a variable that can return only T or nil
fld	Variable representing the file descriptor for an ASCII file accessed by AutoLISP
fun	AutoLISP or user-defined function
fuzz	The maximum difference between two terms for which the equal function will return T
item	**Car** of an association list
lst	AutoLISP list containing strings, numbers, or coordinates
mod	1) Numerical value representing the style of formatting linear dimensions/angles in the UNITS command or the value of the OSMODE variable 2) Alpha representation of selection method
nam	[Path] + name + file extension assigned to an ASCII file
num	Integer or variable representing "counting" number
pat	String with optional wildcards used as search target
pmt	Prompt message string
precision	Number of decimal places returned by string representation of real number
pt	Variable representing a point list, or the point list itself
s/v/v	String, numeric value, or variable representing either one
ss	Selection set—the entities selected by any of the selection options such as Window, Last, etc.
str	String (enclosed in double quotes), or a variable representing a string
sym	1) Variable name before being assigned a value 2) Search target for **tblsearch** function
symu	Name for a user-defined function (UDF)
tst	Arithmetical or logical test expression—returns only T or nil
v/v	Numeric value or variable
v	Variable representing atom, string, or list
val	Value of a system or environmental variable, or a variable representing that value

If only one value is present in the – function, the value is multiplied by minus one. Multiplication and division functions containing a single value will return that value.

Note: The second atom is required for **+** function.

Logical symbols

(sym s/v/v s/v/v [s/v/v...])

sym   One of the following, =, /= (not equal)*, >, <, >=, <=

This function returns T if each atom satisfies the logical relationship with respect to the atom on its right, and nil otherwise.

Note: **/=** is undefined if more than two atoms are present.

(~ v/v)

v/v   Must be integer.

This function returns the bitwise complement of v/v. Loosely speaking, ~ converts num to a binary, then changes the 1s to 0s and vice versa. The result is converted back to base 10 and negated.

(1+ v/v)

Adds one to v/v.

(1- v/v)

Subtracts one from v/v.

(abs v/v)

Returns absolute value of v/v.

(ads)

Returns a list of currently loaded AutoCAD Development System (ADS) applications.

(alert str)

Displays a dialogue box with the message embodied in str and an OK button to accept it.

(alloc num)

Sets memory space for num of nodes.

(and expr expr . . .)

Returns T if none of the expr are, or evaluate to, nil.

(angle pt1 pt2)

Returns the value, in radians, of the angle that a 2-D line from pt1 to pt2 makes with the current horizontal axis. If the points are not at the same elevation, this function returns the results of projecting the points onto the current construction plane.

(angtof str [mod])

Converts a string representing an angle displayed according to the mod setting into a floating point (real) value in radians. If mod is omitted, the current AUNITS setting is assumed. **Angtof** is the complement of **angtos.**

(angtos angle [mod [precision]])

Converts an angle in radians to a string, according to the mod setting. If mod and precision aren't specified, the current settings of AUNITS and AUPREC are used. **Angtos** is the complement of **angtof.**

(append expr expr . . .)

expr Must be in the form of a list.

Runs two or more lists into a single list. Quoted and evaluated lists may be used interchangeably.

(apply fun lst)

Executes fun on arguments supplied by lst.

(ascii str)

Returns the first character of str as an ASCII integer character code. **Ascii** and **chr** are complements for one-character strings.

(assoc item lst)

item Must be quoted ' (to prevent evaluation) **car** of dotted pair.
lst Must be an association list.

Returns the entry in lst that is associated with the specified item.

(atan num1 [num2])

Returns an angle whose tangent is equal to num1 or, if num2 is present, num1/num2. In the first case, the returned value lies between –90 degrees and 90 degrees. In the second case, the value returned will be a positive or negative angle in the quadrant specified by the signs of num1 and num2.

(atof str)

Converts str into a real number.

(atoi str)

Converts str into an integer.

(atom v)

Returns nil if v/v is a list and T if it is not.

(atoms-family fl [lst])

fl   Specifies the format of return. If fl is set to 0, a list of symbols is returned. If fl is set to 1, a list of symbols as strings is returned.

lst   List of symbols to be returned.

This function returns a list of built-in and user-defined symbols specified in lst. Undefined symbols return nil instead of their name. This function is to determine whether a specified UDF is defined in the current drawing.

Note: **atoms-family** replaces the pre-Version 12 **atomlist** function.

(boole fun num1 num2 . . .)

num   Must be integer.

fun   A value determined from the following truth table. The value is 8 if the binary representation of both num1 and num2 is 0 in a given position. If only num1 is 0 in the specified position, the value is 4; if only num2 is 0, the value is 2: and if neither num has a 0, the value is 1. The values may be added, so that a value of 6 will represent the situation where either num1 or num2 (but not both) has a 0 in the position of interest.

Boole is a general-purpose binary function. It compares two binary numbers, position by position. If the two terms satisfy the condition specified by fun, a 1 is entered in the corresponding position in a third binary number; otherwise, a 0 is entered. When all the terms of num1 and num2 have been compared, the third binary number will have as many bits as the largest of num1 or num2. This number will be converted to base 10 and returned by the function.

Logand, **logior**, and **lsh** are also available to evaluate binary numbers. The first two examine corresponding positions of two or more numbers, recording a 1 if the bits in that position satisfy an and/or. The function then returns the decimal representation of 1 bits thus found. **Lsh** moves each bit a specified number of places to the left or right, and is the equivalent of multiplying or dividing the number by a power of two.

Boole may be used in the evaluation of complex logical expressions. However, other functions such as **and**, **not**, and **or** are available for simpler situations.

(boundp atm)

Returns T if atm is bound to any value except nil.

(cal expr)

Invokes AutoCAD's geometry calculator, evaluates expr, and returns the result.

(car lst)

Returns the first element of lst. If lst is empty, returns nil.

(cdr lst)

Returns everything in a list except the first element. **Cdr** returns a list except where lst is a dotted pair, or when lst is empty. In the former instance the returned element is an atom, not a list. In the latter case, nil is returned.

car and cdr derivatives (e.g., (caadr lst))

These functions are compounds of **car** and **cdr**. They consist of combinations of up to four As (for **car**s) or Ds (for **cdr**s) enclosed between a leading C and a trailing R. Application of these functions to empty lists returns nil.

(chr num)

num   Must be an integer.

Converts the integer to the corresponding ASCII character. **Chr** and **ascii** are near complements.

(close fld)

Closes the file specified by fld and returns nil.

(command [arguments])

arguments   The arguments supplied to this function must consist of inputs satisfying the requirements of AutoCAD commands. If the inputs are AutoCAD commands, options, or data, they must be between double quotes. Unquoted inputs in the form of AutoLISP variables or functions (with parentheses) may also be used.

Command may be instructed to pause for user input by including PAUSE at the appropriate places in the command arguments. If a return is required by keyboard input, a pair of double quotes should be inserted in the argument list. AutoCAD's DTEXT and SKETCH commands, which require keyboard input, may not be used inside the **command** function, nor may AutoLISP's GETXXX commands. If the arguments are omitted, **command** will cancel a previous AutoCAD command called from the AutoLISP command function.

(cond tst1 exp 1 [tst2 exp2 . . .])

This function evaluates each test in turn until one returns T. The corresponding res is evaluated and the result returned as the function is exited.

(cons new_element lst*)

new_element   If a variable, must be preceded by a single quote to prevent evaluation.

This function adds the new element to lst producing a longer list. If the first element is a list, the result will be a compound final list with the first element list being the first item in the final list.
    Note: If lst is replaced by an atom, the resulting list will be a dotted pair.

(cos v/v)

v/v   Numerical values must always be in radians.

This function returns the cosine of v/v.

(cvunit v/v str1 str2)

v/v   May also be a list.
str   Must be found in the file "ACAD.UNT".

Converts v/v from the unit specified by str1 to the unit specified by str2.

(defun symu lst expr . . .)

lst Must be a list of arguments for function enclosed in parentheses. Parentheses must be present, even if no arguments are needed.

This is the function used to define user-defined functions (UDFs). Arguments may be global (in which case their values cannot be changed by the function), local (in which case their values *can* be changed within the function), or undefined. Undefined arguments are not included in the argument list and their values can be changed by the function.

   Note: If **symu** name is the same as an AutoLISP symbol or an existing UDF, the former meaning will not be accessible. If **symu** name begins with C:, the resulting UDF may be called by entering it at the command line. If the **symu** does not have an initial C:, it must be placed between parentheses to call it.

(distance pt1 pt2)

Returns the distance between points one and two. If the points differ in elevation, the distance is the 2-D distance between the projections of the points on the current construction plane.

(distof str [mod])

str   Must be compatible with specified mod. If no mod is given, the string must be readable in terms of the current LUNITS format.

Converts the string value of a distance into a real number in either the specified mod or the current value of LUNITS.

(entdel enam)

Deletes entity specified by enam. If the entity was previously deleted during the current drawing session, using **entdel** on it will undelete the entity.

(entget enam [lst])

lst   Must be a list of application names.

Returns the definition data for the entity specified by enam.

(entlast)

Returns the entity name of the last undeleted main entry in the database.

(entmake [lst]*)

lst   Must be an entity list similar to that returned by **entget**, containing all the data required to define the entity. If terms such as *layer* or *text style* are omitted, the default values are used. The −1 entry may be omitted; if it is supplied, AutoLISP ignores it.

Note: The list is optional in the sense that some data can be omitted from its content, but the list itself is required. Nondefinitional data can be omitted, but the basic data on an entity, such as its type (0 group) and location (10, 11, or 40 groups, depending on type) must be supplied by the list.

(entmod lst)

lst   Must be an entity data list.

Updates the data contained in the entity list, thus modifying the drawing of the entity. Although **entmod** may be used on complex entities such as plines and blocks, certain precautions are required. Consult the **entmod** entry in the *AutoLISP Reference* for details.

(entnext [enam])

Returns the entity name of the first undeleted entry in the data list. If enam is supplied, **entnext** returns the name of the first undeleted entry *after* the supplied enam.

(entsel [pmt])

Returns a list consisting of the entity name and the coordinates of the point used to pick it. Entity selection must be done by a single point. Use (**car** (**entsel** pmt)) to obtain the entity name in a form useable by functions such as **entnext**.

(entupd enam)

Ensures that complex entities such as blocks and polylines get properly drawn on the screen after **entmod** is used on them. **Entupd** may (and should) be used on all entities after their databases are modified.

(eq expr1 expr2)

Returns T if both entities are bound to the exact same object. If expr1 and expr2 are bound to different objects of identical form and value, **eq** returns nil.

(equal expr1 expr2 [fuzz])

Returns T if the two expressions differ from each other by less than the value of fuzz. If fuzz is omitted, **equal** is the equivalent of the = function.

(*error* str [expr . . .])

A user-defined error-handling function. The function can only take one argument—the string issued by AutoCAD when a program error arises—but any number of other AutoLISP expressions may be included inside the function.

(eval expr)

Evaluates expr and returns its value.

(exit)

Forces the current program to quit, returns an error message, and returns to the AutoCAD command prompt.

(exp v/v)

v/v   Must be, or evaluate to, a number.

Returns the value of the constant *e* raised to the num power — the antilog of ln num.

(expand num)

Allocates memory node space by requesting num segments.

(expt v/v1 v/v2)

Raises the base (v/v1) to the specified power (v/v2).

(findfile nam)

nam   Must be the name of a file. Directory/drive paths and file extensions may be included.

This function searches the AutoCAD library path and returns the fully qualified file specified by nam. The current directory is first searched, followed by the directory of the current drawing file, the directories specified by the AutoCAD environment variable, and the directory containing the AutoCAD program files. If no file extension is supplied, AutoLISP will disregard extensions in the search. If a drive/directory path is supplied, AutoLISP will search only that directory.

(fix v/v)

Converts v/v into an integer.

(float num)

Converts num into a real number.

(foreach v lst expr . . .)

Steps through lst assigning each member of lst to v in turn, then evaluates the expressions using the current value of v. The value of the last expression is returned. Since all values except that of the last expression are lost, **foreach** is best used for printing a list of outputs.

(gc)

Forces a garbage collection, which frees up unused nodes, thus increasing the available memory space. AutoLISP performs an automatic garbage collection when needed, so this function is normally not required.

(gcd num1 num2)

num Must be integer.

Returns the greatest common denominator of num1 and num2.

Note on All GetXXX Functions: User input to AutoLISP programs is available through **getxxx** functions. These functions provide a real-time link between AutoCAD drawings and the AutoLISP functions used with them. In general, **getxxx** functions are more forgiving than other AutoLISP functions in terms of accepting input. They are, however, subject to some limitations.

AutoLISP functions (including other **getxxx** functions) may not be used directly to supply input to **getxxx** functions. Use **setq** to assign the return from the first function to a variable, and use the variable to supply input to the **getxxx** function.

Some functions, such as **getfiled** and **getenv,** are not **getxxx** functions in the sense used here. These functions may be distinguished from the user-input functions by the absence of any provision for a prompt in their definitions.

(getangle [pt] [pmt])

Accepts user input of angle and returns value in radians. Input may be from keyboard or screen. If optional pt is included, a ghost line from pt to the present cross hair location will appear. The value returned by **getangle** will depend on the current settings of ANGDIR and ANGBASE.

(getcorner pt [pmt])

Accepts 2-D input to obtain a corner, defining a box whose diagonal corner is pt.

(getdist [pt] [pmt])

Returns distance between two points. If optional pt is present and is a 3-D point, a 3-D distance will be returned unless the setting of **initget** prevents 3-D entry.

(getenv str)

str   Must be the quoted name of a system environment variable.

Returns the name and path of a system variable.

(getfiled title default ext num)

ext   The default file extension string.

This function allows the user to select a file from a display box or a keyboard. The dialogue box has the specified title and contains a list of files with the specified default name and ext. (The null string "" may be used for either of these and would be the equivalent of * in the DOS Dir command.) The value of num is a number derived from a binary code. If the zero bit (value 1) is set, a new file will be created. The one bit (value 2) disables the "Type it" button in the box, the two bit (value 4) allows the user to override the setting for ext in the function, and the three bit (value 8) performs a library search for the entered file if the one bit is not set.
   Getfiled is not a **getxxx** type function.

(getint [pmt])

Allows user to input an integer between –32,768 and 32,767.

(getkword [pmt])

When used in conjunction with **initget**, allows control of users' string entries.

(getorient [pt] [pmt])

Similar to **getangle**, except returns are unaffected by the settings of ANGBASE and ANGDIR.

(getpoint [pt] [pmt])

Returns 3-D point. If optional pt is supplied, a rubber band line is created between pt and the current cross hair position.

(getreal [pmt])

Returns a real number.

(getstring [fl] [pmt])

Returns a string. If fl is present and has previously been defined as anything but nil, the string can contain spaces and must be terminated by hitting the Enter key. If fl is nil or absent, data entry may be terminated by hitting the space bar.

(getvar nam)

nam   Quoted name of an AutoCAD variable.

Returns the value of the specified AutoCAD variable.

(graphscr)

Switches from text to graphics screen in single-screen systems. No effect on two-screen systems. **Textscr** is the complement of graphscr.

Note on All Grxxx Functions Except **Grclear**: These functions provide direct access to the screen and input devices. They are dependent on AutoCAD code, which may change; there is no guarantee they are upward-compatible. In addition, unless used exactly as specified in the current version of the AutoLISP reference manual, they may not work in all configurations. In short, stay away from them unless you are a real computer expert!

(grclear)

Clears the current viewport (flipping to the graphics screen if currently in the text screen). The viewport may be restored by using the **redraw** function or the REDRAW command.

(grdraw pt1 pt2 color [highlight])

color   The number representing the desired color.
highlight Any character except 0.

Draws a vector from pt1 to pt2 in the specified color. If highlight is present, the line is drawn and highlighted by the default method of the display device (usually dashed or colored).

    Note: The line drawn by **grdraw** is *not* an AutoCAD entity and cannot be accessed by AutoCAD's LIST or ERASE commands, so it can't be edited or removed from a drawing. The REDRAW command will, however, remove it from the screen.

(grread [track] [allkeys] [curtype])

track   Any non-nil character.
allkeys An integer from 1 to 15 controls input.
curtype An integer from 0 to 2 controls cursor display.

Allows direct input to AutoLISP from AutoCAD input devices such as tablets and menus.

(grtext [box text [highlight]])

box   An integer between the values of 0 and the highest screen menu box minus 1.

This function writes the specified text in the specified screen menu box. If highlight is present and a positive number, existing text written with **grtext** will be highlighted. If box is set to –1, the text will be written in the layer status line area of the screen. Setting box to –2 writes to the coordinate status line area. Calling **grtext** with no arguments restores all on-screen text areas to their standard values.

(grvecs lst [trans])

lst   A list consisting of a series of optional color integers and two-point lists with a format as follows:

([color num] (from pt1)(to pt1)[color num2](from pt2)(to pt2) . . .)

trans   A transformation matrix that allows the location or proportion of the vectors to be changed.

This function allows multiple lines to be drawn on the screen. The conditions are the same as those for **grdraw**.

(handent handle)

Once enabled, entity handles remain associated with the entity even after exiting from the drawing editor. Entity names, on the other hand, are associated with entities only during the duration of a single editing session. **Handent** relates an entity handle to that entity's name so that the latter may be used to access the drawing's data list.

(if tst exp1 [exp2])

If test evaluates as T, then exp1 is evaluated. If not, exp2 is evaluated. If exp 2 is present, the program moves on.

(initget [num] [str])

Initget serves as a filtering function for all the **getxxx** functions. Num gives bitwise control of numerical input, and str allows preset strings to be entered with aliases.

(inters pt1 pt2 pt3 pt4 [fl])

Returns the intersection of the line defined by pt1 pt2 with the line defined by pt3 and pt4. If fl is present and is nil, the lines are treated as if they were infinite; otherwise, the intersection must occur on one of the specified lines.

(itoa v/v)

v/v   Must be, or evaluate to, an integer.

Converts an integer into a string.

(lambda arguments expr . . .)

This function defines an anonymous function. It is useful for situations where the overhead of defining a function with **defun** is not justified, or where the programmer wishes to clarify the logic of a function by laying it out at the point of use.

(last lst)

Returns the last element in a list.

(length lst)

Returns the number of elements in a list.

(list a/l [a/l . . .])

Takes any number of atoms or lists, evaluates them, and forms a list containing them. Variables must have a single quote in front of them if they, rather than their values, are to be listed.

(listp v/v)

Returns T if item is, or evaluates to, a list; nil if otherwise.

(load nam [on failure])

nam   Name of a file of LISP functions between double quotes, with a path but without the .LSP extension.

When a file is loaded into a program, it is evaluated, and the programs in the file may be used by the drawing. If, for any reason, the file doesn't load, it causes an AutoLISP error unless an optional string, atom, is supplied by the on failure entry.

    Note: Whenever a drawing is called up by NEW or OPEN, AutoCAD will automatically load a file called ACAD.LSP if it exists. Any AutoLISP programs on this file will be available to the drawing without having to use the **load** function.

(log num)

Returns the natural log of num.

(logan numd num...)

Returns an integer representing the logical bitwise AND of the numbers. See the discussion on the **boole** function for details.

(logior num . . .)

num   Must be an integer.

Returns an integer representing the logical bitwise OR of a list of numbers. See the discussion on the **boole** function for details.

(lsh num1 num)

num   Number of binary positions to be shifted.

Returns logical num bitwise shift of num1. If num is positive, shift is to the left; if num is negative, shift is to the right. If a one-bit is shifted into or out of the top bit, num1's sign is changed.

(mapcar fun lst1 [lst2 . . .])

Applies the fun to each member of each of the lists, returning a list of the results.

(max v/v v/v [v/v . . .])

Returns the largest of the numbers given. Result is real if any v/v is a real number.

(mem)

Displays the current state of AutoLISP's memory.

(member expr lst)

Searches list for first occurrence of expr, returns a list consisting of the expr and everything after it.

(menucmd str)

str   Must be in the form "menu section=submenu."

Switches individual sections of AutoCAD's menu.

(min v/v v/v [v/v . . .])

Returns the smallest of the numbers given. Returns real number if one or more real numbers are given.

(minusp v/v)

Returns T if v/v is negative or evaluates to a negative quantity.

(nentsel [pmt])

Similar to **entsel** when applied to any entity except a polyline or a block. If applied to a polyline, supplies information on the segment selected. If applied to a block, supplies information on the entity embedded in the block.

    Note: When applied to a block, **entsel** returns a matrix that will enable the transformation of the entity's data points from an internal system relative to the block to the world coordinate system.

(nentselp [pmt] [pt])

Similar to **nentsel,** except for the optional point which allows selection without user input.

    Note: The transformation to the world coordinate system in **nentselp** differs from the method used in **nentsel**. The technique is discussed in the *ADS Programmers Reference* on page 37.

(not expr)

Returns nil if expr is not—or doesn't evaluate to—nil, and T if it does.

(nth num lst)

Returns the num item in the list with num for the first item in the list 0.

(null expr)

Returns T if expr is bound to, or evaluates to, nil.

(open nam mod)

mod   Operation to be executed on file. "w" write, "r" read. "a" append. Letters must be quoted and in lowercase.

Opens a file for input or retrieval of data and returns file descriptor. If the file doesn't exist and mod is "w" or "a", it will be created.
    Note: If the file descriptor is "captured" by assigning it to a variable with **setq**, the variable can be used to access the file.

(or expr . . .)

This function scans the expressions and returns T if any are non-nil.

(osnap pt mod)

mod   An AutoCAD OSNAP option in the form of a quoted string.

Returns the point that would be returned by the OSNAP command if the cross hairs were at pt.

(pi)

A predefined constant with a value of 3.141592 . . . .

(prin1 [expr [fld]])

If fld represents a valid, open-for-writing file, **prin1** prints expr exactly as it appears on the screen. If fld is absent, expr is printed on screen. Control characters (e.g., \n) are printed but do not affect the appearance of the output. Control characters presented as numerical arguments for **chr** are expanded (e.g., (**chr** 10) prints as "\n").

Note: Expr argument need not be a string.

(princ [expr [fld]])

Similar to **prin1,** except control characters are not expanded when present as numerical arguments for **chr**. If, however, control characters are present in their expanded form (e.g., "\t"), they will affect the appearance of the output.

Note: If no argument is present, **princ** returns a blank space, rather than nil. If it is used as the last statement in a program, **princ** will assure a clean exit with no messages cluttering up the command area.

(print [expr [fld]])

Similar to **prin1**, except it prints a new line before expr and a space after it.

(progn expr . . .)

This function groups expr, evaluating each one sequentially and returning the value of the last expr. **Progn** may be used to evaluate several expressions where only one is expected, such as in the **if** function.

(prompt pmt)

Prints pmt on screen prompt area and returns nil.

(quit)

Forces current application to quit and returns to AutoCAD's Command prompt.

(quote expr)

Returns expr unevaluated. When used in a program, may be replaced by ' symbol.
   Note: When used, the quote symbol is placed in front of the leading parenthesis.

(read str*)

Reads the first list or atom in str. The argument is returned as the appropriate numeric or string data type.
   Note: String cannot contain spaces unless contained between \" control characters (e.g. "\"First message\"").

(read-char [fld])

Reads a single character from keyboard input buffer or open file and returns ASCII code for that character. If used repeatedly, **read-char** "steps" through a string, reading a new character each time it is called.

(read-line [fld])

Reads a string from a file that is open for reading. Returns line, unless end-of-file marker is encountered, in which case it returns nil.

(redraw [enam [mod]])

mod 1 redraws entity; *mod* 2 blanks out entity; *mod* 3 highlights entity; *mod* 4 unhighlights entity.

If called with no arguments, it redraws current viewport. If called with enam, it redraws the entry as specified by mod value.

(regapp application)

Registers an application name with the current drawing. This enables drawing to use external programs that access extended entity data.

(rem v/v1 v/v2 . . .)

v/v   Must be, or evaluate to, a numerical value.

Divides v/v1 by v/v2, then divides the remainder by num3 . . .. If none of the numbers is real, the result is an integer.

(repeat v/v expr . . .)

v/v   Must be integer quantity.

Repeats expr v/v times.

(reverse lst)

Returns list with the last element of lst in the first position of the returned list, the next-to-last element of lst in the second position, etc.

(rtos num [mod [precision]])

mod   Corresponds to settings for UNITS command.

Converts a real number to a string in a format specified by mod and with the specified precision. If the optional entries are omitted, **rtos** follows the current settings of the LUNITS and LUPREC system variables.

(set sym* expr)

sym   Must be quoted with ' or **quote**.

Sets the value of sym to expr.

Note: If sym is not quoted, **set** can indirectly assign a value to any other symbol represented by sym. For this reason, limit the use of **set** to those situations where it is necessary to evaluate sym in order to assign it a value.

Warning: Do not use **set** to assign values to AutoLISP functions.

(setq sym1 expr1 [sym2 expr2 . . .])

Sets the value of each sym to its corresponding expr.

Warning: Do not use **setq** to assign values to AutoLISP functions.

(setvar system variable val)

Sets a system variable to a specified value.

(sin v/v)

v/v   Angle in radians.

Returns the sine of an angle.

(sqrt v/v)

Returns the square root of v/v as a real number.

(ssadd [enam [ss]])

If called alone, **ssadd** creates a new, empty selection set. If called with enam and ss, enam is added to ss.

(ssdel enam ss)

Deletes entity specified by enam from selection set.

(ssget [mod] [pt1] [pt2] [lst] [filter-list])

mod   Selection mode in quotes or "X".

If used alone, **ssget** prompts the user to select entities using AutoCAD's selection procedure and places them in a selection set. If mod is present and requires screen input, the pick points must be specified with pt1/pt2 (for "W" or "C") or lst (for "WP", "CP", or "F"). If the "X" mode is used, the entire database is scanned; otherwise, selection is limited to entities on the screen.

Filters may be used in conjunction with entity data lists to limit the selection of entities to specified types, sizes, or properties. Various relational operators are available to construct the necessary filter lists.

(sslength ss)

Returns the length of the specified selection set.

(ssmember enam ss)

Returns enam if the entity is a member of the specified selection set; nil if it is not.

(strcase str [fl])

Returns a copy of str with alphabetic characters converted to upper- or lowercase depending on fl. If fl is missing or evaluates to nil, string is returned with uppercase characters; otherwise it is returned with lowercase characters.

(strcat str1 str2 [str3 . . .])

Returns a string that is the concatenation of the supplied strings.

(strlen str [str . . .])

Returns the total length of the string(s) as an integer.

(subst new old lst)

Returns a copy of lst with new substituted for every occurrence of old.

(substr str num [length])

Returns a length-long substring of str, starting at position num (first character of string is number 1). If length is omitted, return string runs from character n to the end of str.

(tablet code [row1 row2 row3 direction])

code   If 0, function returns current calibration; if 1, the row and direction values must be present.

This function establishes a relationship between points on a digitizer and the screen, for use when the tablet mode is enabled for copying drawings. The row values establish a 3×3 matrix for a transformation, and the direction value is a 3-D point that establishes a normal to the plane that represents the surface of the tablet.

(tblnext table-name [fl])

table-name   Upper- or lowercase string representing the name of one of the tables listing AutoCAD's named entities. Valid names are: "Layer", "Ltype", "View", "Style", "Block", "UCS", "Appid", "Dimstyle", and "Vports".

Returns the data list (as a list of dotted pairs, without the –1 group) of an entity in the specified table. If used repeatedly, **tblnext** steps through each entry in the table. If fl is present and doesn't evaluate to nil, the first entry is returned each time the function is called.

(tblsearch table-name sym [[fl])

This function searches a named table for the specified sym. If it is found, the function returns the same type of data list as **tblnext**; otherwise, it returns nil. If fl is set and non-nil, the entry counter is adjusted so that a subsequent **tblsearch** starts at the entry after the one returned by the previous search.

(terpri)

Prints a new line on the screen and returns nil.
   Note: Works with file I/O.

(textbox elst)

elst   Entity list for a text entity. At the minimum, the list must include the one-group list. The complete entity list must be enclosed in parentheses with a leading **quote** or **'**.

Measures a text entity and returns the diagonal coordinates of a box that encloses the text. The text is treated as if it is horizontal and its insertion point is 0,0,0. Regardless of the text orientation, the first point returned is always the lower-left corner of the enclosing box; the other point is the upper-right.

Note: Since **textbox** always returns a horizontal box with its lower-left corner offset from a 0,0 insertion point, the box can only be drawn directly for horizontal text inserted at 0,0. The best approach to drawing boxes around aligned, fit, or left-justified text with other insertion points or nonhorizontal orientation is to draw the box using the coordinates returned by **textbox,** then move it from 0,0 to the text's left insertion point and rotate if necessary. If other types of justification are used, the box will have to be located by eye.

(textpage)

Switches from a single-screen installation's graphics screen to a cleared text screen.

(textscr)

Similar to **textpage,** except screen is not cleared. **Textscr** is equivalent to hitting the switch screen key in AutoCAD.

(trace fun1 [fun2 . . .])

A debugging aid. When invoked, **trace** sets a flag for the specified functions. Each time one of the functions is evaluated, a display appears showing the function and its value.

(trans pt from to [fl])

from/to   The initial and final coordinate systems displayed as:

   a. An integer code. 0 = WCS, 1 = Current UCS, 2 = Display coordinate system, 3 = Paper space display coordinate system (used only with code 2).

   b. An entity name (entity coordinate system).

   c. A list of three real numbers indicating an extrusion direction.

Translates a point or displacement from one coordinate system to another. If fl is present and non-nil, pt is treated as a 3-D displacement vector rather than a point.

(untrace fun1 [fun2 . . .])

Turns off **trace** for the specified function(s).

(vmon)

This function is not needed in AutoLISP for Version 12, but is retained to provide compatibility. It enables virtual function paging.

(vports)

Returns a list of viewports for the current configuration. Each viewport is numbered with the current one listed first, and the dimensions of the viewport are given as if the screen's coordinates ranged between 0,0 and 1,1.

(wcmatch str pat1 [pat2 . . .])

pat   A quoted string that may contain wildcards, including the following:

    #   a numerical

    @   an alphabetic character

    *   any character sequence

    ?   any single character

    ~   anything *except* the pattern, if first character in pattern

    [. . .] any character enclosed

Note: Multiple patterns may be used if separated by commas.

Returns T if str matches any one of the patterns.

(while tst expr . . .)

Evaluates tst. If it is not nil, evaluates all other expr, then repeats until tst evaluates to nil.

(write-char num [fld])

num   Must be the ASCII code for a character.

Writes character represented by num to screen or open file (if fld present).

(write-line str [fld])

Writes a string to the screen or open file specified by fld.

(xdroom enam)

Returns the amount of extended entity data space that is available for the specified entity.

(xdsize lst)

lst   Must start with an application name that has previously been registered with **regapp** followed by the extended data. Lst, itself between parentheses, must be enclosed by a second set of parentheses.

The size (in bytes) that lst occupies when it is appended to an entity as extended data.

(xload application [on failure])

application   The quoted name of an existing AutoCAD development system application.

Loads an ADS application. If application does not load, the function returns an AutoLISP error or the on failure argument.

(xunload application [on failure])

application   The quoted name of a previously loaded ADS application.

Unloads an ADS application. If unloading is not successful, and the on failure argument is present, it is returned instead of AutoLISP error message.

(zerop v/v)

Returns T if v/v is or evaluates to 0. Otherwise, returns nil.

APPENDIX B

Solutions to Exercises

Chapter 1   Exercise 1

```
(command "LINE" pt1 pt2 ""
         "ARRAY" "L" "" "P" pt1 12 "" ""
)
```

Command functions can be stacked, so the coding can be grouped between a pair of parentheses. Once you realize that the LINE and ARRAY commands are called for, the coding is relatively direct except for one thing. Did you remember to put in the quotation marks to terminate LINE, the entity selection, and the defaults for 360 degrees and object rotation in ARRAY? Most AutoCAD users are so used to accepting defaults and terminating commands with a return that they forget that AutoLISP requires double quotes.

Chapter 1   Exercise 2

The first thing to realize about this exercise is that your results will depend on how you made the list. If you made it with **quote,** the list will be ("ART" "bob" chuck d2), but if you made it with **list,** your result will be ("ART" "bob" nil nil). This illustrates the essential difference between the two list-building functions. **Quote** or ' returns the input verbatim, as does **list** in the case of strings or numerical quantities. The difference is in the way the two functions handle nonquoted "strings." When **list** is supplied with an alphabetic or alphanumeric sequence of characters, it assumes that it is looking at a variable unless the sequence is enclosed in quotes (which signify a string). **List** will return the *value* of a variable, not just the name of the variable, and when the value has not been assigned, **list** returns nil. **Quote**, on the other hand, returns exactly what was fed to it.

Once a list has been established, there's no way to switch the list itself from literals to values. For example:

```
(setq x 1 y 2 z 3)
(setq a (quote (x y z))
      b (list a)
)
```

will return the compound list ((x y z)). If **quote** and **list** were interchanged in the above coding, *B* would return *A*, without evaluation. Entering "!a" at the command prompt would produce (1 2 3).

Assuming that the list was made with **quote**, **car** *A* returns "ART", the first member; **cdr** *A* would return the rest of the list as a list—("bob" chuck D2). To get "bob" you need the **car** of the **cdr** of *A* or **cadr** *A*. **Cddr** would give you (chuck D2). You can again get the first term by taking the **car** of the modified list, giving you the **car** of **cddr** *A* or **caddr** *A*. Using the same technique, **cdddr** of *A* returns the one-atom list (D2), and taking the **car** of that, or (**car** (**cdddr** *A*)) (which could be written (**cadddr** *A*)) will return D2. The required terms are listed below:

(**car** *A*) returns "ART"	(**cadr** *A*) returns "bob"
(**caddr** *A*) returns chuck	(**cadddr** *A*) returns D2

If the list was formed with **list**, the **caddr** and **caddr** of *A* would both return nil.

Chapter 1   Exercise 3

List *B* contains two sublists, (1 2 3) and (4 5 6). **Car** *B* returns the first item in list *B*, (1 2 3), and **cdr** *B* returns the second item as a list within a list ((4 5 6)). To get the first three items of a list you normally use **car**, **cadr**, and **caddr**. In this case, though, you can't apply them to the whole list, *B,* since the atoms you want are part of the sublist (**car** *B*). This means that to extract the first X coordinate, you need the **car** of **car** *B*, or **caar** *B*. To extract the other two coordinates, take the **cadr** and **caddr** of **car** *B* respectively, which would be **cadar** *B* and **caddar** *B*.

To get the individual coordinates for the second point, you first have to extract the point list from list B by taking the **car** of the **cdr** or **cadr** *B* to get the simple list (4 5 6). Then, following the same procedure as you did for the first point, take the **car** of **cadr** *B*, the **cadr** of **cadr** *B*, and the **caddr** of **cadr** *B*, giving you **caadr** *B*, **cadadr** *B*, and **caddar** *B*, respectively. This would work for the X and Y coordinates, but if you type "(caddadr)" at the command line, you would get an "error: null function" response! Why? To see what's happening, first enter **cddar** B. That returns the list (3), a list containing the third atom of the first point list. If you enter **cddadr** B (notice the last "D"), the list (6) will be returned. This corresponds to what happened with the first point list—you got a list with the Z coordinate of the point. Now, to extract the first item from a list, take the **car** of the list. Try it the long way: (**car caddar** B)) returns 3, and (**car** (**cddadr** B)) returns 6! We've gotten the Z coordinate of the second point. But if **caddar** B worked for the first point, why didn't its equivalent **caddadr** B work for the second point? Take a closer look at the two functions. First, strip the **c** and the **r** from them, leaving **adda** and **addad**. Now you can see the reason: remember, you can only nest **car** and **cdr** functions four deep and **caddadr** is asking for *five* levels. In fact, if you "translate" **caddadr** working from left to right, you'll see what it is calling for (the underlined items represent what is returned at each step):

> **a** the first item <u>6</u>
>
> **d** from a list containing everything but the first item from (<u>6</u>)
>
> **d** a list containing everything but the first item from (<u>5 6</u>)
>
> **a** the list (<u>4 5 6</u>)
>
> **d** a list containing everything but the first item of B ((<u>4 5 6</u>))
>
> B ((1 2 3) (4 5 6))

That's too much to keep track of, even for a computer, but if you look at the individual lines, you can see that **d** always returns a list, while **a** can return either a list or an atom.

To sum up:

(**caar** B) returns 1; (**cadar** B) returns 2; (**caddar** B) returns 3; (**caadr** B) returns 4; (**cadadr** B) returns 5; (**cddadr**) returns (6); and (**car** (**cddar**)) returns 6.

Chapter 1   Exercise 4

There are a number of ways of accessing a long list besides stacking up **car**, **cdr**, and their derivatives. The simplest technique is to take the **car** of the list (Sun in this instance), then redefine the list as the **cdr** of itself. This means that the list is now (Mon Tue Wed Thu Fri Sat), and the **car** of the revised list is now Mon. By repeating the process, you can strip the list of each leading item in turn. One problem with this approach is that the original list will be destroyed, but by assigning the list to a new variable (e.g., *XC*) and stripping the new list, the initial list can be retained.

The **nth** function is another approach. To extract all the items from the list, a loop may be set up with a counter that is incremented from 0 to n–1 (where *n* is the number of items in the list) for each pass. Using **nth** allows more selectivity than stripping. For example, (nth 3 C) will return Wed without going through Sun, Mon, and Tue. An alternate approach would be to use seven separate **nth** functions, with counters ranging from 0 to 6 to assign values to seven different variables.

If the last item of in the list is the only one of interest, it can be extracted using **last** or by combining **car** and **reverse**. Using **reverse** also allows the programmer to use functions such as **cadddr** to access the end of a list without stacking.

Chapter 1   Exercise 5

list V	lst OK	&list A	AplusB A	A+B V	A_B A
NEWLIST A	POINT1 OK/A		PT1 OK	CIRCLE V	DiA OK
OLST OK					
NUM(1) V	FIVE% OK				

NUM(1) uses reserved parentheses, A+B uses a reserved plus sign. CIRCLE and LIST are AutoCAD and AutoLISP commands respectively. PT1, DiA, OLST, and lst are perfectly acceptable. &list, A_B, FIVE%, and AplusB are acceptable, but could be confusing because nonalphabetic symbols are usually unexpected. In addition "AplusB" will show up as "APLUSB" in AutoLISP messages. NEWLIST should be avoided because it exceeds six letters.

That leaves "POINT1." If it is in the same program as PT1, it could cause confusion. If PT1 isn't in the same program, why go through the trouble of hitting three extra keys?

Chapter 1   Exercise 6

27 is an integer.
"27" and "TWENTY-SEVEN" are strings.
27.0 is real.
.27e+02 and 27. are incorrect because the decimal point either begins or ends the number.
27E2 is an acceptable real representation of 2700.0.
270/10 is incorrect—AutoLISP will not perform operations on data. Of course, if given 270 and 10 as separate data entities, it will do operations *with* them.
"TWENNY-SEVEN AND A HALF" is a good string—spelling doesn't count!
(27) is incorrect as data; it is a list.

Chapter 1   Exercise 7

Either of the following is acceptable:

```
(setq a 1 b 2 c 3 d 4 e 5)
```

or

```
(setq a 1
      b 2
      c 3
      d 4
      e 5
)
```

Be sure you put the function between parentheses and that you use spaces and/or line feeds to separate each of the atoms. If you use the second technique, the alignment isn't critical.

The **set** function could have been used, but if it was, each variable a–e must have a single quote (') in front of it to prevent the function from trying to evaluate the variables instead of assigning values to them.

Chapter 1   Exercise 8

The basic ways of making the list would be (list a b c d e) or '(a b c d e). In the latter case, the function could be spelled out, giving (quote a b c d e). Using the **list** approach, you would produce the list (1 2 3 4 5). Using either ' or **quote**, the list produced would be (a b c d e). You must use the **list** function if you want the *values* of literals. This being the case, (list '(2 3) '(4 5)) would return an acceptable list of lists, but (quote (list 2 3) (list 4 5)) would return an error message. Strangely, (quote (list 2 3)) would return (list 2 3), which would return (2 3), a list. But why bother with the compound list (quote (list 2 3)) when the simple list (list 2 3) would accomplish the same thing?

Chapter 1   Exercise 9

The **setvar** function is used to set system variables. The syntax is (setvar "VARIABLE" value). The variable name must be in quotes. The value is usually a number, and if it is, need not be quoted. Most of the system variables with string values are "Read only" so **setvar** can't be used on them. In the few cases, such as CLAYER, where the value can be set with AutoLISP, it too must be in quotes.

The correct response to this question is:

```
(setvar "SNAPMODE" 1)
(setvar "gridmode" 1)
```

Notice that **setvar**, unlike **setq**, cannot be stacked. Only one variable name and value can be associated with each **setvar**. (The same applies to **setvar**'s clone **getvar** which returns system variables' values.) The system variable's name may be in upper- or lowercase.

Chapter 1   Exercise 10

As disappointing as it may be, your name is just another string to AutoLISP, therefore, the function to use is **getstring**. The syntax for **getstring** is: (getstring flag "prompt"). If you entered something like "(getstring T "Name")", your input would be terminated when you hit the space bar to separate your first and last names. The reason for this is the requirement that the flag, "T" in this case, not only must be present, but also be assigned a non-nil value. If T or its equivalent were not previously assigned a value with a **setq** function, it would return nil, so **getstring** would not accept space in its input. Therefore, to get your name assigned to the variable NAME, use coding similar to that below:

```
(setq T 1
    NAME (getstring t "Enter your name ")
)
```

Enter your name at the prompt, and hit return when you're finished.

Chapter 1   Exercise 11

Getint will accept 5, but will return a "Requires an integer value" message for .3 (a real), and "two" (a string).

Getreal will return "Requires numeric value" for the string, but will return 5.0 (real) and a properly formatted 0.3. Remember, inside the program, reals must always have a digit before and after the decimal point.

Getstring will return a string value for anything entered, so all inputs will be between quotes. However, if you remembered that two was a string and supplied "two" to **getstring**, the return string would be ""two""—which could cause trouble later (see Chapter 6).

Chapter 2   Exercise 1

The best way to work this type of problem is to follow the algebraic practice of working from the inside out.

1. Get the product of 4, A, and C: (* 4 A C)
2. Square B by using (expt B 2) or (* B B)
3. Subtract the product (– (expt B 2) (* 4 A C))
4. Take the square root of the combined term:

```
(sqrt (- (expt B 2) (* 4 A C)))
```

5. Get the negative of B: (– 0 B) or (– B)
6. Add it to everything else:

```
(+ (- 0 B) (sqrt (- (expt B 2) (* 4 A C))))
```

7. Double the value of A: (* 2 A)
8. Divide the expression in 6 by 2A

```
(/ (+ (- 0 B) (sqrt (- (expt B 2) (* 4 A C)))) (* 2 A))
```

Chapter 2   Exercise 2

Either the flow is equal or greater than 7, or else it isn't. In the first case, the pipe diameter is 1.25, otherwise it is .875. Expressed this way, it should be clear that the **if** function should be used.

```
(if (>= FLOW 7)
    (setq DIA 1.25)
    (setq DIA 0.875)
)
```

Don't forget the leading zero.

Chapter 2   Exercise 3

```
(setq POWER 7
      TEMP TEST)
```

```
(repeat (1- POWER)
    (setq TEMP (* TEMP TEST)
  )
  (setq TEST TEMP)
```

In situations such as this, you can't just use TEST inside the loop. If you did, TEST would be squared seven times, and you would end up with the fourteenth power instead of the seventh. Using TEMP as a placeholder allows you to use simpler coding. If you wanted to raise TEST to a different power, just change the value of POWER. Subtracting one from POWER when setting the **repeat** counter permits the user to set the power directly and eliminates the possibility of forgetting that you need only loop n – 1 times to raise to the nth power.

Chapter 2   Exercise 4

Since the object of this exercise is to reach a certain value for a series of operations, we must program to stop at the value, rather than after a specific number of cycles. The function to use is **while**, and the coding is:

```
(setq num 1
      prod 1
(
(while (< prod 1250)
    (setq prod (* prod num)
          num (1+ num)
    )
)
(setq num (1- num))
```

The program will cycle until PROD equals or exceeds 1250, then it will exit the **while** loop. During the cycle, before PROD causes an exit, the value of NUM is increased by one in preparation for the next cycle. This means that the value of NUM upon exiting will be one more than the largest number whose factorial is less than 1250, so it will have to be reduced to satisfy the problem's requirements. This situation frequently occurs when you're using the results of an operation in a loop.

Be sure not to include the initial assignment statements for any variables whose values will be changed inside the loop. If you do, no matter what happens as the loop progresses, your values will be initialized whenever the loop repeats. Check this out by moving the first **setq** inside the loop—you'll see that both NUM and PROD will be reset to 1 at the start of each cycle.

Chapter 2   Exercise 5

Both **if** and **cond** can be used whenever you have a known number of test conditions and you wish to take different actions depending on the state of each condition. As the number of possible conditions increases, programming with the **if** function becomes more complex and the **cond** function becomes the method of choice. In the present instance, we have four possible results, so **cond** is set up with three actual **Test** statements (which will return T, if true), and one statement that will always return T. This approach guarantees that there is an exit from **cond** even if an unexpected condition should arise. (Consider, for example, what would happen if DIR had a value of "North".) The problem with this approach is that improper input will not be detected by the **cond** statement and could corrupt the program's output. This can be avoided if steps are taken to limit the input to acceptable values.

The coding for the problem is:

```
(cond
    ((= dir "N") (setq pt '(0 1)))
    ((= dir "W") (setq pt '(-1 0)))
    ((= dir "S") (setq pt '(0 -1)))
    ( T (setq pt '(1 0))
)
```

Chapter 3   Exercise 1

You can write this program using an undeclared variable for the input. Redefine the value using **cond** and stack **setq**s to set both the numerical and string values.

```
(defun METRIC ()
    (cond
        ( (<= a 0.0394)
            (setq a (* a 25.4)
                unit "mm"
            )
        )
        ( (and (> a 0.0394)(<= a 0.3937))
            (setq a (* a 2.54)
                unit "cm"
            )
        )
        ( (> a 0.3937)
```

```
(setq a (* 0.0254 a)
      unit "m"
)
  )
)
```

Since any value for *A* will satisfy one of the conditions, there is no need to force the last condition to return T.

Since both *A* and *UNIT* were undeclared, both were available when the UDF was over. Because *UNIT* was the last evaluation in the function, it could have been declared local and its value captured by enclosing the function between the parentheses of a **setq**. The second approach would conserve the limited memory allocated to store AutoLISP variables (since *UNIT*'s space would be released upon exiting from **metric**), but only if an existing variable were available to hold *UNIT*'s value.

Chapter 3   Exercise 2

The midpoint of P1–P2 could be found by finding the average of the **car**'s and **cadr**'s of the endpoints and using them to form the point list of P3. A more direct approach would be to use **osnap** in the MIDpoint mode set to either P1 or P2.

Once P3 was established, the required line could be drawn with **polar** with P3 as the starting point, **angle** P1–P2 minus pi/2 as the angle (remember angles must be supplied in radians), and the specified distance between P3 and P4.

```
(setq p3 (osnap p1 "MID")
      p4 (polar p1 (- (angle p1 p2) (/ pi 2)) dist)
)
```

Remember to supply the value of P1 as the first argument for **angle**. Otherwise the function would return the reverse angle, and P4 would be on the wrong side of P1–P2.

Chapter 3   Exercise 3

You'll investigate the handling of defaults at prompts in a later chapter. For now, you can just work with a simplified model. All AutoLISP default values are in the form of strings and must be converted to numerical values if they are to be passed on to a **command** function as numerical input, so a data conversion problem exists. On the other hand, if you convert all the string inputs to real numbers with **atof**, you can always convert the output from your code to integers with **fix** when integer input is required. This will save you the trouble of coping with the real/integer problem within your code.

The only remaining problem is to find out what character or characters are returned when you hit the return key in response to an AutoLISP prompt. You can check this out for yourself by entering something similar to "(setq x (getint "Prompt "))" at the command line, hitting the return key, then finding the value of x by entering !x and getting nil as the "value."

Now, with all the questions answered, you can do the coding. There are two ways to handle the default situation; the first method uses **if** to directly assign a value to *VAL*:

```
(setq val (getxxx "Prompt <DEF> "))
(if (= val nil)
    (setq val (atof def))
)
```

If the return key is entered at the prompt, *VAL* will be assigned a value of nil and the **if** function **Test** expression will return T. The **Then** condition will be implemented and the default will be supplied. If a value is entered, the **Test** condition will not be satisfied, so the **if** function will do nothing and the value assigned by the **setq** will stand.

The second approach to handling a default involves embedding an **if** inside a **setq** and using the value returned to set *VAL*.

```
(setq qrs (getxxx "Prompt <DEF> ")
      val (if qrs qrs (atof def))
)
```

The key to this approach is the second line. If a value is assigned to *QRS*, the **if** function returns that value, which is then assigned to *VAL*. If the first line returns nil (which is *not* a value), **if** returns *DEF*, which is equated to VAL.

One final point. **Getxxx**, a generic user-input function, was used to emphasize the point that both of these approaches could be used for real, integer, or string inputs. (In the last case, the **atof** function would be omitted and the string "" rather than nil would be returned.) This can be done because "nil" is acceptable input for any numerical input function and will not be rejected when generated by the Enter key. Typing in nil in response to a **getreal** prompt will bring up an error message.

Chapter 3   Exercise 4

This exercise is intended as practice for handling arguments, so using undeclared variables in the UDF is counterproductive. The required coding is:

```
(setq a "string 1" b "string 2" c "string 3")
(UDF a b c)
```

where UDF is defined by the code:

```
(defun UDF (x y z) (list x y z))
```

The real fun comes when you try to make UDF run with only two arguments. You end up with an error message because once a function is defined with arguments (or symbols), they must be supplied whenever the function is called. In this case, since we are dealing with strings, you could supply a dummy argument with a call such as:

```
(udf "" b c)
```

If the function were numeric in nature you would have to either supply 0 or 1 depending on whether addition/subtraction or multiplication/division were involved. If the operations within the function included, for example, multiplication and subtraction of the missing variable, they would have to be rewritten to eliminate the variable, since no single numerical value would be neutral.

We sometimes resort to using functions with dummy arguments to avoid having to rewrite complex specialized functions. Most of the time though, it isn't worth the trouble. If we keep our UDFs short and simple, we can build complex programs by using elementary functions as building blocks. That way, if we have to modify the program we can make the appropriate changes in the relatively simple UDFs, without having to tear apart the entire complex structure.

Chapter 4

The solutions given below represent only one of several possible approaches to each problem. If your answers differ, check them out by setting up the necessary variables at the command line then entering your code.

Chapter 4   Exercise 1

This is our old friend, the rectangle program, slightly disguised. With the rectangle, we picked two points, and used them to derive the other two points. Here, we need only pick one point, since the other points are each one unit away from the previous one at an angle increasing pi/2 radians for each segment.

```
(setq a (getpoint "Pick point: ")
      a90 (/ PI 2)
      a180 PI
        b (polar a 0 1)
        c (polar b a90 1)
        d (polar c a180 1)
)
(command "LINE" a b c d "C")
```

You could also use the relative coordinates in the **command** function. If you do, remember that they must be entered in the AutoCAD format, between quotes (i. e., "@1,0").

Chapter 4   Exercise 2

This is a simple one. Assume that the desired layer is CON. The code would be:

```
(command "CHPROP" "L" "" "LA" "CON" "")
```

Don't forget the paired quotes to end the selection process and the command itself.

Chapter 4   Exercise 3

In this case, since the basic coding is already in place, the easiest approach is to modify it. XOFF adds the input to the list. If the input is zero, it terminates the list-building process. You can keep the zero off the list by adding another check inside the loop. Replace the line:

```
dl (cons d dl)
```

in XOFF with:

```
);this closes the stacked setq
(if (/= d 0) (setq dl (cons d dl)))
```

The former closing parenthesis for **setq** now closes off the **if**.

Where the values are entered from the keyboard, **=** may safely be used for the **Test** expression. If input is picked from the screen, or if division is used to derive the value, **equal** should be used to avoid rounding errors. If **Test** expressions are used to exit a loop when a specified value is reached, **>=** or **equal** should be used, so that small rounding errors will not prevent an exit due to overshooting the **Test** term.

Chapter 4   Exercise 4

The obvious AutoCAD approach will not work at this time. Yes, LIST will give both the radius and center of a circle, but it will not pass this data on to AutoLISP. Suppose you pick a circle with QUAdrant or NEAr OSNAP active and use the point so picked in AutoLISP's **osnap** function with CENter active? In that case, you'd have two points, the initial pick, P1, and the center, P2. **Distance** would give you the radius.

AutoLISP permits us to use OSNAP modes within **setq**s, for instance:

```
(setq b (osnap a "MID"))
```

would either give the midpoint of the entity located at or near point *A* or, if no midpoint could be found, return a nil value for *B*. In this case, a **getpoint** function has to be used to pick point P1. You can't use OSNAP because the **getxxx** function's syntax doesn't allow for a quoted term. This means that in order to use an OSNAP when you pick the point inside a program, OSNAP's mode must be set prior to your use of the **getpoint** function. This may be done either by using OSNAP in a **command** function, or by setting the system variable *OSMODE* to either 16 for QUAdrant or 512 for NEAr with the **setvar** function. You can avoid the issue by setting OSNAP before you start coding.

The problem then is getting the circle's radius and drawing either a circumscribed hexagon or octagon around the circle's center.

```
(setq p1 (getpoint "Pick a circle: ");QUA or NEA already set
      p2 (osnap p1 "CEN")
      rad (distance p1 p2)
)
(if (= rad 0.755)
  (command "POLYGON" 6 p2 "C" 0.755)
  (command "POLYGON" "8" p2 "C" ".805")
)
```

Notice that in the first **command** statement, the numerical values were not quoted, so AutoLISP interpreted them as AutoLISP input. The corresponding values were quoted in the second **command** statement, so they were fed as input to AutoCAD. Either method is acceptable, but if you choose not to quote, remember that real numbers must have embedded decimals.

Chapter 4   Exercise 5

Here you have three possibilities: the radius is within 0.002 of 0.805, the radius is within 0.002 of 0.755, or it is some other value. You could use a string of **if** statements to handle this problem, but the **cond** statement will allow you to do it more directly. The tests and **command** statements for radii of .755 and .855 resemble the ones used in Exercise 4, except **equal** with a fuzz factor of 0.002 is used in place of =. If neither of these conditions is satisfied, the third possibility must be true. The code for that situation is:

```
(T (command "CIRCLE" p2 "1"))
```

which, if it is reached, will draw a one-unit radius circle instead of a polygon around the given hole.

Chapter 4   Exercise 6

Assume that the length, width, and height are assigned to the variables *L*, *W*, and *H*. The front view will be an *L* by *H* rectangle; the top view, *L* by *W*; and the right-side view, *W* by *H*. Given a starting point, each rectangle may be drawn using coding similar to that used for Exercise 1 and explicitly coding in the lines. An alternative would be to locate the upper-right corner of each rectangle in terms of the appropriate variables added to the starting point's **car** and **cadr** functions. Since the starting point for the front rectangle is known to be 1,.5, the other starting points may be derived as follows:

```
(setq spf '(1 0.5)
      spr (list (+ L 2 (car spf)) (cadr spf))
      spt (list (car spf)(+ H 2 (cadr spf)))
)
```

The code for the front rectangle is given below as an example. Coding for the other rectangles is up to you.

```
(setq p3 (list
            (+ (car spf) L)(+ (cadr spf) H)
            )
      p2 (list (car p3)(cadr spf))
      p4 (list (car spf)(cadr p3))
)
(command "LINE" spf p2 p3 p4 "C")
```

Since the coding to draw the individual rectangles differs only in the starting point and the given dimensions involved, it would be relatively easy to convert it to a UDF and save yourself the trouble of writing another 16–20 lines of code.

Chapter 5   Exercise 1

If the only requirement is to avoid specifying boxes with X and Y coordinates greater than 10.5 and 7.5 respectively, the coding below will be satisfactory.

```
(setq x (getreal "Enter X coordinate < 10.5: "))
    (if (> x 10.5)(setq x 10.5))
(setq y (getreal "Enter Y coordinate < 7.5: "))
    (if (> y 7.5)(setq y 7.5))
```

If the object is to force the user to specify a point and still satisfy the conditions of the exercise, coding like the following should be used.

```
(setq x 12.0)
(while (> x 10.5)
    (setq x (getreal "Enter X coordinate < 10.5: "))
)
```

If too large a value were entered for the X coordinate, the program would repeat the loop, and the user would be prompted for a new value.

If **car** and **cadr** were used with **getpoint** in a **while** loop, the user would be able to pick a point from the screen. With this approach, an **or** would be used in the **Test** expression.

Chapter 5   Exercise 2

If the programmer doesn't take into account all the conditions that could cause an AutoCAD command to receive improper input from an AutoLISP program, the program could crash. This behavior doesn't exactly encourage users to rely on AutoLISP programs or programmers, so it is best not to make any assumptions about the AutoCAD environment when setting up an AutoLISP program.

If a nonexistent layer is called for in a **command** function, the function will be canceled and the program will crash. A crash will also occur if the New option of the LAYER command is invoked to create an already existing layer. No crash will occur if an attempt is made to create an existing layer with LAYER's Make option.

Although AutoLISP has functions that will check AutoCAD to see whether named entities such as text styles, blocks, and layers exist, these functions are too advanced to be covered here, so we'll have to attack the problem in another way. Let's assume that the layer we want to switch will be named "CON1", is red, and has continuous lines, but has not been created when we invoke our program for the first time. The following code will create the layer, move the entities to that layer, and set a flag so that subsequent calls to the program will merely change the entities.

```
(if (= flag "set")
    (command "CHPROP" "W" pause pause "" "LA" "CON1" "")
    (progn
    (command "LAYER" "M" "CON1" "C" "R" ""
             "CHPROP" "W" pause pause "" "LA" "CON1" "")
    )
    (setq flag "set")
    )
)
```

Unfortunately, because of the explicit pause statements, the user can only input two points; in this case, the corners of a window. In Chapter 6 we will see how AutoLISP can be programmed to inform the user of what selection options are available.

If the first line of this program had read "(if flag)", (meaning if a variable named *FLAG* existed and had been assigned a non-nil value), the program would have acted on the first command statement. The trouble with this approach is that if the variable *FLAG* had been used for any purpose in the current drawing session, it would still have its last value, so the new layer wouldn't be created. All in all, it is better to play it safe and assign your test variable a value within your program.

Chapter 5   Exercise 3

This exercise requires you to build a list of point lists and keep track of the number of entries so you can draw the appropriate number of line segments. You have to change a system variable for the duration of the program and then change it back to its starting value.

```
(setq old (getvar "OSMODE")
      count 0
        lst (list) ;dummy list
)
(setvar "OSMODE" 35);changes POINT type
(while (or pt (= count 0))
      (setq msg "Select point or hit return to exit: "
              pt (getpoint msg)
          count (1+ count)
            lst (cons pt lst)
      )
)
(repeat (1- count)
     (setq p1 (car lst) p2 (cadr lst) lst (cdr lst))
     (command "LINE" p1 p2 ""
              "POINT" p1
     )
)
(command "POINT" p2)
(setvar "OSMODE" old)
```

After the first point is selected, the count is no longer zero, so the **while** statement is controlled by the input to *PT*. Upon exiting from the **while** loop, the program enters a **repeat** loop. The first line selects the first two-point list from *LST*, then redefines it by removing the first sublist. The **command** function draws a line between the given points, exits the line command, and puts a point on P1. On the next pass, the first two points from the redefined *LST* (the second and third points from the original list) are selected and the process is repeated. When the **repeat** loop is satisfied, the program places a point on the last P2 and resets OSMODE to its initial value.

Chapter 5   Exercise 4

Use **getpoint** and **getreal** to get *PT* and *DIA* representing the center and diameter of each circle. Put the values into a sublist using **list**, and into the master list by again using **list**. The techniques used in Exercise 3 will enable you to set up a counter and terminate the input phase of the program.

Use the value of the counter in a **repeat** loop. Extract each sublist using **car** and redefine the master list using **cdr**. Extract the values of *PT* and *DIA* from each sublist. The code below will do the rest.

```
(setq dia (/ dia 2))
(if (= typ hex)
     (command "POLYGON" "6" pt "C" dia)
     (command "POLYGON" "8" pt "C" dia)
)
```

This program is similar to the one in Chapter 4's exercises, except in this case, the user enters the specifics of the circle, while in Chapter 4, the user had to find these quantities. The method of choice depends on the starting condition of the problem, and the programmer should be flexible enough to consider both approaches before starting to write code.

___

Chapter 5   Exercise 5

If the hole shows as a circle in the front view, it will show as two parallel lines offset by the circle's diameter in both views. Since the length, width, and height of the rectangles are known and represented by the variables *L*, *W*, and *H*, and the space between rectangles is known to be two units, the location and length of each line can be determined. In the end view, for instance, the lower, hidden line will start at a point where the X coordinate is the lower-left corner of the front view (1) plus *L* plus 2, and the Y coordinate is one radius below the center of the circle in the front view. The line will be *W* units long.

For the purpose of this program, assume that the lines will be drawn on an existing layer called "HID" with a hidden linetype.

```
(setq ola (getvar "CLAYER");gets current layer
      oos (getvar "OSMODE");current osnap mode
)
(setvar "CLAYER" "HID")
(setvar "OSMODE" 512);NEArest
(setq p1
  (getpoint "\nSelect point on circle in front view: ")
      p2 (osnap p1 "CEN")
      rad (distance p1 p2)
      dia (* rad 2)
      xs1 (+ 1 L 2);X coordinate side view start
      ys (- (cadr p2) rad);Y coordinate side view
      xs2 (+ xs1 W);X coordinate side view end
```

```
        sp (list xs1 ys);start point
        se (list xs2 ys);end point
     mid (list (/ (+ (car sp)(car se)) 2)(cadr sp))
)
(command "LAYER" "S" "HID" ""
         "LINE" sp ep ""
         "OFFSET" dia mid p2 ""
)
```

This coding will draw the line representing the bottom of the hole in the end view and offset it to produce a line representing the top. The coding for the representation of the hole in the top view has the following changes: *XS1* would be **car** of P2; *YS1* would be (+ 0.5 H 2); and *YS2* corresponding to *XS2* would be the sum of *YS1* and *W*. In addition, since the layer was previously set, it would not have to be set to "HID".

When all four lines have been drawn or offset, the variables should be reset to their initial values:

```
(setvar "CLAYER" ola)
(setvar "OSMODE" oos)
```

Chapter 6   Exercise 1

The best thing to do in a situation like this is to rewrite the program so that the user doesn't need a screen full of instructions. A program that requires extensive instructions to the operator is poorly written. The user's options in a program should be limited, and each choice should be programmed in, so that user input is minimized. Sometimes, though, there isn't time to do the extensive programming that this approach requires. If reprogramming can't be done, supply a printed handout to be used with the program. As a last resort, and to satisfy the conditions of the exercise, use the approach below.

```
(textpage);switches to an empty text screen
(prompt "FIRST 256 CHARACTERS OF MESSAGE")

(prompt "LAST 256 CHARACTERS OF MESSAGE")
(princ); prints blank line at the end of message
;|The line below will let the operator study the message as long
as needed, then go on to the rest of the program.|;
(setq x (getstring "\nHit any key to continue"))
```

You will probably have to play around with the text, so that words aren't split between two lines. Given the fact that you may have to retype your entire message several times to make it readable on the screen, you can see why this approach should only be used as a last resort.

Chapter 6   Exercise 2

Assume that you want to input a CIRCLE centered at 3.5, 2 with a 1.25 diameter. The data can be written to a file as follows:

```
(setq a "CIRCLE" b '(3.5 2) c "D" d 1.25 e ",")
(setq out (open "TEST.TXT" "w"))
(princ a out)(princ e out)
(princ b out)(princ e out)
(princ c out)(princ e out)
(princ d out)(prin1 out);prints blank line
(setq out (close out))
```

To extract the data, the file must be reopened, this time for reading.

```
(setq out (open "TEST.TXT" "r"))
(setq ln (read-line out))
```

The returned line will read:

```
"CIRCLE,(3.5 2),D,1.25"
```

This is a string, with commas in the seventh, fifteenth, and seventeenth positions.

A program similar to ROUT which was discussed in this chapter could be used to extract each entry as a string, then **read** could be used to convert the numerical terms. Variables representing the resulting expressions may be fed to a **command** function.

As an alternative, the data may be extracted by using **substr** to break out each term and **read** to convert the numeric terms.

```
(setq m (substr ln 1 6);"CIRCLE"
      n (read (substr ln 8 7));list (3.5 2)
      o (substr ln 16 1); "D"
      p (read (substr ln 18 4));1.25
)
```

Using these entries, the circle may be redrawn with:

```
(command m n o p)
```

Chapter 6   Exercise 3

In this case, the **substr** approach would be the easiest to work with. Be sure to allow enough space for all the entries for each entity.Use extra lines if necessary.

Chapter 6   Exercise 4

This program will pick two consecutive vertices of a hexagon going in an anticlockwise (CCW) direction. Using **distance** and **angle** on the two points thus picked, you can determine the length of the hexagon's side and its orientation.

If lines are drawn from the center of a hexagon to two consecutive vertices, an equiangular triangle will be formed. The line from the second point (going CCW) to the center will form an angle of 120 degrees (2*pi/3 radians) more than the angle that the side makes with a horizontal line drawn through the first vertex. Since all sides of an equiangular triangle are equal, the length of the center–vertex line is the same as that of the vertex–vertex line. The center of the polygon can then be located using the **polar** function. If OSNAP were set to End, the following code could be used for the accession section:

```
(setq msg1 "\nPick a vertex: "
      msg2 "\nPick the next (CCW) vertex: "
      pt1 (getpoint msg1)
      pt2 (getpoint msg2)
      dist (distance pt1 pt2)
      ang (angle pt2 pt1)
      angp (+ ang (* 2 (/ pi 3 )))
      cen (polar pt2 ang dist)
      rad (dist)
)
```

In the more general case, lines from the center of a regular n-sided polygon to two adjoining vertices form triangles with the center angle equal to (/ (* 2 pi) n) and two outside angles each equal to one-half of the difference between pi and the center angle. If two points on the ends of one side are known, the triangle can be solved for the other two sides using **cos** and **tan** functions and one half of the distance between the two picked points. The center of the polygon may be found using the same technique as was used for the hexagon. The radius of the circumscribed circle is equal to the hypotenuse found with the **sin** function, and that of the inscribed circle is equal to the length of the remaining side.

Chapter 7

The discussions below generally deal with methods for solving the accession sections of the exercises. This was done because, at this stage, if you can program the accession section, you are probably capable of programming the other sections as well.

In order to show the logic of the programs more clearly, UDFs have not been used. If you followed the suggestion given when outlining these exercises, you've used UDFs in your programs. If you haven't made wide use of UDFs, go through your program again. In general, if you have to go through a procedure more than once or twice, it is worth your time to handle the procedure with a UDF.

Chapter 7   Exercise 1

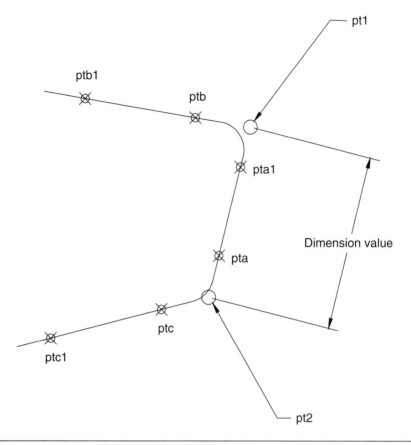

EXERCISE 7.1

The problem arises in this case because the intersections of the line to be dimensioned and its neighbors have been lost as a result of drawing the fillet or chamfer. If all the lines involved were either horizontal or vertical, the intersection could be found by setting up a point with the .Y coordinate of a horizontal line and the .X coordinate of a vertical, but in general, this solution would not work.

The **inters** function, when supplied with two points for each of the lines involved with the intersection, will supply the coordinates for an intersection no matter the orientation of the two lines. You can establish the intersection by setting OSNAP to Endpoint and picking points as follows:

```
(setq msg1 "\nSelect the line to be dimensioned. "
      msg2 "\nSelect an adjoining line. "
```

```
        msg3 "\nSelect the other adjoining line. "
        pta (getpoint msg1)
        ptb (getpoint msg2)
        ptc (getpoint msg3)
      pta1 (osnap pta "MID")
      ptb1 (osnap ptb "MID")
      ptc1 (osnap ptc "MID")
      flag nil
        pt1 (inters pta pta1 ptb ptb1 flag)
        pt2 (inters pta pta1 ptc ptc1 flag)
)
```

The three **getpoint** picks supply the endpoints of the lines involved. The three **osnap** functions use the endpoints to get the midpoint of each of the lines. The first intersection (PT1) is established by supplying two points from the line to be dimensioned and two points from the first adjoining line to **inters**.[1] By replacing the first adjoining line's points with the second's, PT2, the second intersection is obtained. Taken together, PT1 and PT2 represent the endpoints of the line before the fillet or chamfer was applied.

Once PT1 and PT2 are available, an automatic dimensioning program may be invoked to determine the type of dimension line needed and to supply the starting point for the extension lines.

Chapter 7 Exercise 2

The program is required to break a selected line, insert a 0.5 × 0.5 unit block at a 1:1 scale and zero degree rotation, and supply a value to an attribute prompt. Assuming that the name of each block is the same as the name of the component it represents, and that OSNAP is set to NEAr, this may be accomplished by the following code:

```
(setq nam (getstring "\nComponent: ")
      lab (getstring "\nLabel:      ")
      ip (getpoint "\nInsertion point: ")
)
(command "BREAK" ip "@1,0"
         "INSERT" nam ip "" "" 0 lab
)
```

---

[1]Because the optional *FLAG* was set to nil, the lines were treated as if they were infinite. If it were not previously assigned a value, *FLAG* would be nil, but you can't be sure that it hasn't already been assigned a non-nil value. Explicitly assigning the nil value was just playing it safe.

Chapter 7   Exercise 3

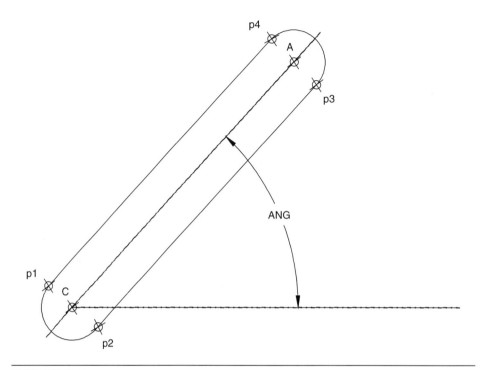

EXERCISE 7.3

Using the operator-supplied values for the center of the left arc (*C*), and the length and angle of the slot (*A*), the center of the right arc is determined. The starting and ending points for the top line (P1 and P4) are established from *A* and *C* using **polar**, the angle of the slot plus $\pi/2$, and the half-width of the arc. The corresponding points for the bottom are found in a similar manner, except in this case, $\pi/2$ is subtracted from the slot's angle.

```
(setq msg1 "\nPick the center of the left hand arc: "
      msg2
       "\nEnter the center-to-center length of the slot: "
      msg3 "\nEnter angle slot makes with horizontal"
      msg4 "\nEnter width of slot: "
        c (getpoint msg1)
      len (getdist msg2)
      ang (getreal msg3)
      wid (/ (getreal msg4) 2)
        a (polar c ang len)
       p1 (polar c (+ ang Pi) wid)
```

```
        p2 (polar c (- ang Pi) wid)
        p3 (polar a (+ ang Pi) wid)
        p4 (polar a (- ang Pi) wid)
)
```

With the endpoints of the slot's entities established, the first arc is drawn. Then the lines and the other arc are drawn using the Continue option of LINE and ARC.

```
(command "ARC" p1 "C" a p2
         "LINE" "" p3 ""
         "ARC" "" p4
         "LINE" "" p1 ""
)
```

Chapter 7   Exercise 4

The coding here is similar to that for the previous exercise. It is complicated by the necessity for including information about the angles and by the requirement that the operator be offered two possible ways of laying out the center line of the angle.

If the user indicates the center line by the three-point method, the starting and ending points of the arc will be specified. If the arc is laid out using start point, center, and chord length, the start and center points will be known, but not the endpoint. By deriving the center of the three-point arc, the slot may be drawn the same way, regardless of the method used to draw the center line.

```
(setq rad (/ (getreal "\nWidth of slot: ") 2)
(texpage); brings up empty text screen
(prompt "The center line of the slot may be specified")
( prompt "\n   with either the 3P or SCL method")
(prompt "\n\nIn either case, select start so that arc")
(prompt "\n      is drawn in CCW direction ")
(princ);suppresses nil return from prompt
(initget "3P SCL")
(setq msg
"\nSpecify 3 Point (3P) or Start/Cen/Len (SCL) method: ")
     type (getkword msg)
)
(if (= type 3P)
   (progn
      (setq a (getpoint "\nSelect start point: ")
            b (getpoint "\nSelect second point: ")
            c (getpoint "\nSelect endpoint: ")
```

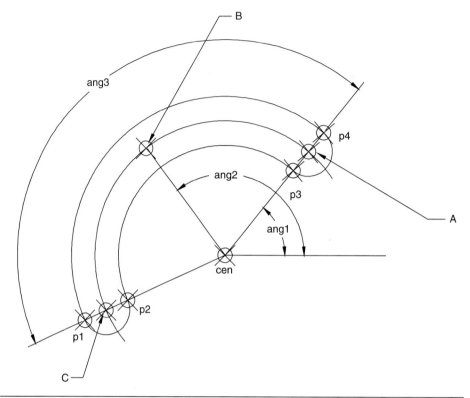

EXERCISE 7.4

```
   )
   (command "ARC" a b c
           "SELECT" "L" "";puts arc in selection set
   )
   (setq b (osnap b "MID");redefines b as midpoint
      cen (osnap b "CEN");center of arc
     ang1 (angle cen a)
     ang3 (angle cen c)
   );close setq
);close progn
(progn
   (setq a (getpoint "\nSelect start point: ")
      cen (getpoint "\nSelect center of arc: ")
      len (getdist "\Length of chord: ")
   )
   (command "ARC" a "C" cen "L" len
           "SELECT" "L" ""
   )
   (setq b (osnap a "MID")
```

```
          ang1 (angle cen a)
          ang2 (angle cen b)
          ang3 (* 2 (- ang2 ang 1))
             c (polar cen ang 3 (distance cen a))
     )
   );close progn
);close if
```

At this point, we have the center (*CEN*), start (*A*), and end (*C*) points for both methods, as well as the center–start (*ANG1*) and center–end (*ANG3*) angles for arcs drawn by either method. Since it isn't needed anymore, we erase the arc. Then we specify the intersection points for the arcs and draw them.

```
(command "ERASE" "P" "")
(setq p1 (polar c ang3 rad)
      p2 (polar c (- ang3 pi) rad)
      p3 (polar a ang1 rad)
      p4 (polar a (- ang1 pi) rad)
)
(command  "ARC" p1 "C" c p2
          "ARC" "" p3
          "ARC" "" p4
          "ARC" "" p5
)
```

If for some reason, you choose not to use ARC's Continue option, you may draw the arcs using the SCE method. Just be sure you specify the points in the proper (CCW) order.

Chapter 8   Exercise 1

A selection set consisting of 0.25 radius circles can be established with a statement such as:

```
(setq a (ssget "X" '((0 . "CIRCLE")(40 . 0.25))
```

Set up five selection sets in this manner one for each radius, using a different variable for each set. Then change the color of each selection set with a **command** function and the **chprop** function, using a different variable name and color name or number each time. For example, given the code above:

```
(command "CHPROP" a "C" 3 "")
```

will make all the 0.5 diameter circles on the drawing green. The **command** functions may be stacked, but if you try to stack the **ssget**s using an incremented variable for the value of the radius, the program will crash. In order to read the variable for the radius, the **quote** function must be replaced by **list**, which will attempt to evaluate the dotted pairs instead of just passing them on.

Since the "X" option of **ssget** scans the drawing's database, any circles satisfying the filter list will be selected. You may elect to use another selection method. This will allow you to use a filter list but permits better control of your selection. Don't forget to set off the "dot" in each dotted-pair sublist with spaces.

Chapter 8   Exercise 2

Build up a selection set using filters to extract the entities with (0 . "DIMENSION") and (1 . 1.25) sublists. Use **sslength** and **ssname** to call up each selected entity in turn, then use **subst** to replace the **cdr** of the 1 group with 1.27. Assuming that the entity's name is *ENT*, the coding should look like this:

```
(setq ent
      (subst (cons 1 "1.27") (assoc 1 ent) ent)
)
(entmod ent)
```

The **cdr** of the second **cons** statement could also be set to "1.25".

Chapter 8   Exercise 3

Instruct the user to pick a line on the top of the figure. Then extract the 10 and 11 groups of the line. If the **cadr** of the 10 group is less than that of the 11 group, the line must be going from left to right, and the figure is drawn clockwise. The only difference between the **autdim**'s procedures for clockwise and anticlockwise figures is that, in the latter, the angle from the midpoint of the line to the "Dimension line location" point is 90 degrees less than the angle of the line instead of 90 degrees *greater*. So, an **if** statement can be used to set the value of the angle used in locating the point.

If you ever decide to use **autdim** on actual drawings, you may want to remove the lines resulting from applying EXPLODE to the polyline to speed up printing. If the polyline were drawn on a unused layer and every other layer was turned off after dimensioning, the extra lines could be removed with an ERASE command and windowing the extent of the drawing. On the other hand, since a selection set with the names of all the lines is available, a more elegant removal procedure would be to step through the selection set and apply **entdel** to each entity.

APPENDIX C

A Final Word

At this point, you should have a pretty good understanding of the basics of AutoLISP. So where do you go now?

Assuming that you want to go on with AutoLISP, the best thing to do is to study existing AutoLISP programs. These are available in many periodicals dealing with AutoCAD. By going through them you can increase your understanding of how AutoLISP works and, more importantly, how other programmers deal with the problems that arise in going from AutoCAD to AutoLISP. Many of these programs, particularly those in *Cadalyst* and *Cadence*, two of the better magazines in this area, may serve as starting points for programs dealing with your own specific problems. Coding for many programs is included with the AutoCAD source code, but some of these are extremely complex, so don't be surprised if you have difficulties in following them. You could also check the AutoCAD User Group on the Internet.

Since this book was written with the intent of bringing readers up to speed so that they could write their own application programs, elegance in programming has been sacrificed for simplicity. If you really want to get into good AutoLISP programming, knowledge of some of the other programming languages, such as C or C+ and Pascal, will give you a better feel for what constitutes good programming practice. The C programming language, in particular, has many applications in AutoCAD development system (ADS) programming, and is helpful when dealing with complex problems.

If you feel that you've learned enough AutoLISP to handle your day-to-day work, be aware that, unless you frequently apply your programming skills, you'll become rusty with time. The best way to keep your AutoLISP skills is to use them as frequently as possible. Any time that you find yourself working on a sequence of commands that you've used before, you are looking at a candidate for an AutoLISP program. Look at what you've done, and try to write a program to accomplish the same thing. Even if you never actually get around to writing the code, such exercise will serve to keep your AutoLISP skills sharp.

If you do go on with programming, you'll soon be writing programs to solve your own problems. The first program will be rough. You'll probably have to debug it, maybe even completely rewrite it. If you stick to it, though, sooner or later you'll have a program that works. When that happens, you'll get a feeling of accomplishment that will make the whole effort worthwhile.

INDEX

This index covers only those AutoLISP functions and techniques discussed in the main body of the text, excluding programs and program fragments. Page references are given for all functions listed in the tables, and additional references are given for those functions covered by discussions in the text, but no references are given for passing references to a function. Readers wishing information on any AutoCAD v12 functions not discussed in the body of the text should consult Appendix A.

A

arguments. *See* variables
arithmetic functions
    1+ (add one), 25
    + (addition), 25
    / (division), 25
    * (multiplication), 25
    1– (subtract one), 25
    – (subtraction), 25
    abs (absolute value), 25, 26
    exp (exponent of *e*), 25
    expt (exponent of any base), 25
    log (natural log), 25
    max (largest number in list), 25
    min (smallest number in list), 25
    pi, 6, 25, 43
    rem (remainder after division), 25
    sqrt (square root), 25
    zerop (checks for zero value), 25
ASCII (American Standard for Computer Information Interchange)
    character codes, 26
    text/files, 68, 77, 82
        checking, 69, 72
        writing, 68, 69
assignment functions
    set, 10, 11
        compared with setq, 11, 103
    setq, 7, 10, 72
    setvar, 10, 59, 64, 70, 74
atoms, 2